Teaching social skills to youth

Also from the Boys Town Press

BOOKS

Basic Social Skills for Youth
The Well-Managed Classroom
Common Sense Parenting
Helping Teens Unmask Sexual Con Games
The SAY Book: A Program for Sexually Abused Youth
The Ongoing Journey: Awakening Spiritual Life in At-Risk Youth
Working with Aggressive Youth
Preventing Suicides of Youth
Effective Skills for Child-Care Workers
Caring for Youth in Shelters
Sexually Abused Children in Foster Care
What Makes Boys Town So Special
I Think of My Homelessness
Boys Town: A Photographic History

VIDEOS

Common Sense Parenting: Helping Your Child Succeed
Common Sense Parenting: Teaching Responsible Behavior
Videos for Parents Series
Sign With Me: A Family Sign Language Curriculum Series
Read With Me: Storytelling with Deaf Toddlers

To order copies of "Basic Social Skills for Youth" or for a free copy of the Boys Town Press catalog, call **1-800-282-6657**.

Teaching social skills to youth

A curriculum for child–care providers

▶ **by Tom Dowd, M.A.,
Jeff Tierney, M.Ed.**

BOYS TOWN PRESS

BOYS TOWN, NEBRASKA

Teaching social skills to youth

Published by The Boys Town Press
Father Flanagan's Boys' Home
Boys Town, Nebraska 68010

Publisher's Cataloging in Publication

Dowd, Tom.
    Teaching social skills to youth: a curriculum for child-care providers / by Tom Dowd, Jeff Tierney. – 5th printing. – Boys Town, Neb. : Boys Town Press, 1995, c1992.
    viii, 292 p. ; 28 cm.
    Includes bibliographical references (p. 291-292) and index.
    ISBN 0-938510-30-4

    1. Social skills in children – Study and teaching. I. Tierney, Jeff. II. Title.

HQ783.D69 1995   303.32
                            93-159136

Table of contents

Introduction

As human beings, we live in social groups. We learn early in life that there are consequences, both positive and negative, attached to how we interact with others and how we choose to respond in social situations. This process of "socialization," which begins in the earliest interactions between infant and parent, prepares us for more complex situations later in childhood and adolescence. Ideally, lessons learned at each stage in a child's development become the tools that are used to successfully meet the demands of subsequent stages of life.

Today, however, our young people are challenged by an increasingly difficult world. Family problems, substance abuse, economic pressures, and the lure of gangs and delinquency threaten our children physically, emotionally, and spiritually. The tools required to successfully cope with these internal and external pressures include the ability to interact with others in socially acceptable ways and make appropriate decisions in social situations. The focus of this manual is on the development of abilities such as these in children and adolescents, particularly those already at risk as a result of abuse or neglect, emotional or behavioral problems, or difficulties in learning. The curriculum of social skills presented in this manual, as well as the techniques described for teaching these skills individually and in groups, have been used successfully for nearly 20 years as part of a system of youth treatment technology known as the Boys Town Family Home Program, developed at Father Flanagan's Boys' Home in the Village of Boys Town, Nebraska.

▶ Boys Town

Popularly known as Boys Town, Father Flanagan's Boys' Home was founded in 1917 by Father Edward J. Flanagan. Currently under the direction of Father Val Peter, Boys Town's mission remains essentially the same: to provide a safe environment for young people to put their lives in order and, in many cases, heal wounds that run very deep. This is accomplished through four major service programs. The Boys Town Home Campus Program provides care for more than 550 boys and girls in 78 family style group homes located on the original 1,500–acre campus of Father Flanagan's Boys' Home in Nebraska. The Boys Town USA program is spearheading the effort to develop regional Boys Town–owned sites around the country, several of which currently operate in states such as New York, Florida, Texas, and California. The Boys Town Family Based Program provides Crisis Intervention, Parent Training, Shelter Care, and Specialized Foster Care services. Finally, the Boys Town National Training Center provides training, consultation, technical services, and specialized workshops to numerous child–care organizations, residential facilities, and schools across the country. Each program at Boys Town utilizes the Family Home Program model.

▶ The Boys Town Family Home Program

The Boys Town Family Home Program is a philosophy and a method of child care and treatment. The program is based on the notion that the youth it serves have not yet learned the skills necessary to live happy, productive lives. They also may be engaging in inappropriate ways of getting their needs fulfilled because they lack a better behavioral repertoire. This treatment approach focuses on teaching these youth essential life skills necessary for successful transition into young adulthood in a "family style" treatment setting (Peter, 1986). Social, academic, and vocational skills, as well as spiritual values, are actively taught through reinforcement, practice and rehearsal, and a positive style of correction. The social skills contained in this manual are an integral part of this system. The youth are taught behaviors that are thought to be the most functional for them and produce the best long–term rewards. The curriculum of skills and the techniques that are covered here form the cornerstone of treatment planning and active intervention at Boys Town, and can be integrated into a variety of residential and educational environments.

This manual and the accompanying workshop will focus on the development of social skills in children, the elements of social behavior (task and behavior analysis), individual and group teaching techniques, planning skill–based treatment interventions for difficult youth problems, and the format of the Boys Town social skills curriculum. The emphasis will be on viewing social skills training as a pervasive intervention strategy that can be used to address a variety of serious youth issues, including aggressive acting out, depression and suicide, delinquency, and school–related problems. The social skills curriculum defines the positive alternative to many of the maladaptive and self–defeating behavior patterns in which a young person may engage. It is intended to be an effective resource and tool for anyone working with children and adolescents.

CHAPTER ONE

An overview of social skills training

The complexities of human social behavior become readily apparent upon examination of techniques for training a youth to be more "socially skilled." Activities that many people find quite easy (carrying on a conversation, introducing oneself to a guest, etc.) can present major hurdles for a young person who has not developed a repertoire of effective social behaviors and whose deficiencies are compounded by emotional or behavioral issues. In addition, a youth who is capable of demonstrating appropriate social skills still may have difficulty in recognizing when, where, and with whom to use a particular skill.

A youth also needs to learn how to "read" other people's social behaviors and cues. Successful social interactions depend, to a large part, on the ability to perceive and correctly interpret the nonverbal behaviors of others and to demonstrate sensitivity to their points of view and feelings (Hazel, Schumaker, Sherman, and Sheldon–Wildgen, 1983). All of these elements represent a complex social skill structure and level of integration that many youth will not develop without active intervention and teaching from the adults in their lives. This chapter will focus on the concept of social skills, the results of social skill deficiencies, and the importance of social skill training to children and youth with special needs.

▶ The concept of social skills

Social skills, as a concept, can be elusive and difficult to define. In formulating a definition, as well as an approach to teaching social skills, we should consider how the value of a given skill is assessed, and by whom (Combs and Slaby, 1977). The value and meaning of a particular skill actually may be assessed from a number of different perspectives including: 1) the effect on the overall functioning of a group from the point of view of an adult (e.g. the teacher's assessment of appropriate skills for the classroom); 2) the effect on the youth's social standing from the point of view of his or her peers; or 3) the effect on the youth's own feelings of social competence and belonging. Many adults working with children and adolescents neglect to consider the potential discrepancies between these differing points of view. For example, a child's resistance to peer pressure may be considered very important by the adults responsible for his or her care, but may be negatively valued by the child's peer group and result in exclusion and a lowered sense of belonging. In fact, the awareness of peer group values and norms has been consistently found to correlate with peer group acceptance and popularity (Oden, 1980). Therefore, how we define, select, and teach social skills should be considered from the child's perspective, as well as that of the child's caregivers.

One frequently cited definition of social skills that attempts to take into account these differing perspectives refers to a social skill as "the ability to interact with others in a given social context in specific ways that are socially acceptable or valued and, at the same time, personally beneficial, mutually beneficial, or beneficial primarily to others" (Combs and Slaby, 1977). In this sense, social skills are sets of behaviors that do not necessarily remain constant, but may vary with the social context and particular situational demands. These skills also are seen as producing posi-

tive consequences for the individual ("personally beneficial"), but within the norms of societal acceptability and responsiveness to others.

The use of appropriate social skills also represents an immensely complex chain of rapidly occurring interpersonal events. The ability to perform a given skill actually is comprised of several crucial activities occurring nearly simultaneously (Figure 1.1). The socially competent person must: 1) initially be motivated to perform socially appropriate behaviors; 2) be able to perceive social situations accurately and identify which skill to use; 3) be able to decode and correctly interpret information from others; 4) perform the correct verbal and nonverbal responses that make up the skill; 5) be sensitive to social feedback; and 6) be able to integrate that feedback appropriately to enhance social interaction (Hazel et al., 1983). The enormity of this task for a youth with emotional or cognitive limitations is readily apparent. Many youth may have considerable difficulty in organizing and "meshing" their behaviors into smoothly flowing interactions with others, particularly under stressful conditions.

The task of the staff responsible for teaching the youth appropriate social behavior therefore becomes equally complex. This is due, in part, to the act of "learning a new skill" being a skill in and of itself. For the youth to benefit from social skills training, they need to be initially motivated to learn alternative ways of behaving, even if their motivation is external, and they need to be able to keep resistance and noncompliance to a minimum. In addition, each youth would need to have the verbal and motor capacity to

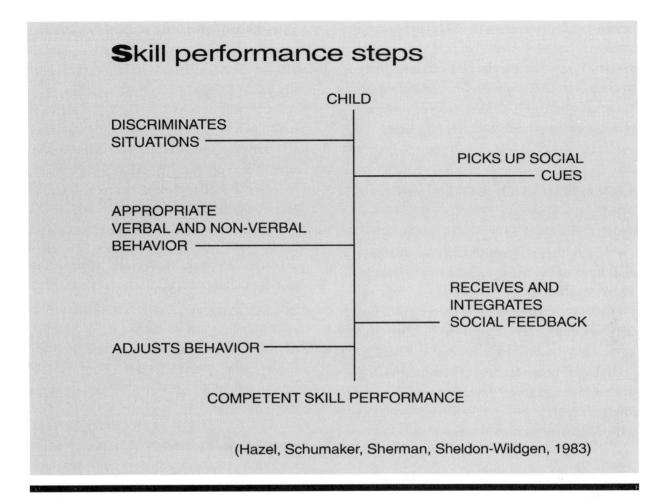

Skill performance steps

CHILD

DISCRIMINATES
SITUATIONS

PICKS UP SOCIAL
CUES

APPROPRIATE
VERBAL AND NON-VERBAL
BEHAVIOR

RECEIVES AND
INTEGRATES
SOCIAL FEEDBACK

ADJUSTS BEHAVIOR

COMPETENT SKILL PERFORMANCE

(Hazel, Schumaker, Sherman, Sheldon-Wildgen, 1983)

Figure 1.1

perform the skill. Staff, on the other hand, must be willing to adjust their techniques, vocabulary, and own interpersonal behaviors to mesh with the learning style of each youth. Finally, the need for social skills training to present meaningful alternatives to a youth cannot be overemphasized. Social skills must have value to a youth, without sacrificing all peer group norms, in order to be learned and utilized in diverse situations.

The philosophy within the Boys Town program regarding social skills instruc-

tion is that problem behaviors demonstrated by a youth are viewed as deficits in the youth's repertoire of these skills and that active, direct instruction is a key to remediation and growth. Positive, prosocial behaviors can be modeled, taught, and rewarded, and, therefore, become viable alternatives for the youth when he or she is confronted with situations that previously resulted in getting into trouble. It has been theorized that adolescents who commit illegal acts do so because they do not have the skills necessary for achieving desired goals through legitimate means, not because of any intrinsic value present in breaking the law (Hazel et al., 1983). For these youth in particular, social skills training may present alternative paths for reaching an acceptable outcome, as well as a viable means of avoiding costly negative consequences.

▶ Correlates of social skill deficiencies

In some youth, deficits in social skill functioning are overt and unmistakable. These youth may be awkward, lack appropriate humor, communicate poorly, etc. But the difficulties encountered by children and adolescents with ineffective social behavior and judgment go far beyond simply feeling uncomfortable in a conversation. The following problem areas have been associated with deficits in social skill functioning:

Correlates of social skill deficiencies

1. Aggressive and antisocial behavior
2. Juvenile delinquency
3. Child abuse and neglect
4. Mental health disorders
5. Loneliness and despondency
6. Learning disabilities and school failure

Figure 1.2

Aggression and antisocial behavior: Numerous indexes of problems in social interaction style have been associated with verbally and physically aggressive behavior in children, including "unpopularity," which has been shown to be a risk factor for delinquency and conduct problems (Kazdin, 1985; Goldstein, Sprafkin, Gershaw, and Klein, 1980). Social skills training has been used to decrease aggressive acting out in adolescent psychiatric patients (Elder, Edelstein, and Narick, 1979) and chronic antisocial behavior in inner–city students (Jones and Offord, 1989). Interpersonal aggression that is used to coerce the behavior of others appears to frequently develop in families that experience external stressors, such as economic disadvantage, combined with a lack of appropriate problem–solving and child management skills (Patterson, 1982).

Juvenile delinquency: The majority of social skills training programs and research has been directed toward juvenile delinquency in adolescents (LeCroy, 1983). Numerous studies have demonstrated a strong link between delinquent behavior and poor social interactional skills (Howing, Wodarski, Kurtz, and Gaudin, 1990; Long and Sherer, 1984; Kazdin, 1985). Institutionalized juvenile delinquents also have been shown to be particularly deficient in social skills "knowledge" (the ability to hypothetically pick the appropriate course of action in a problem situation), with those scoring lowest having the most severe behavioral problems (Veneziano and Veneziano, 1988).

Child abuse and neglect: Strong evidence exists to link the abuse and mistreatment of children, particularly early in life, to later deficits in social functioning (Howing et al., 1990). Abused children have been found to display numerous dysfunctional patterns in their social interactions with adults and peers, including both aggressiveness and withdrawal. Critical social skills training areas for abused children include interpersonal communication, problem–solving, self–control, appropriate assertiveness, and stress management.

Mental health disorders: Mental disorders in adolescents and adults appear to be strongly associated with, and exacerbated by, a lack of social competency and skill (Trower, Bryant, and Argyle, 1978; Kazdin, 1985). It is thought that the social inadequacy accompanying many mental disturbances results in increased social rejection and isolation, thus adding to the original sources of stress and deterioration. For example, one of the areas adolescents in psychiatric settings have been found to be particularly deficient in is conversation skills (Hansen, St. Lawrence, and Christoff, 1988). In addition, children who experience greater amounts of social isolation and rejection also are more likely to experience serious mental health problems in adulthood (Combs and Slaby, 1977).

Loneliness and despondency: A lack of age–appropriate social knowledge and the corresponding rejection by peers seem to be major factors associated with chronic loneliness, isolation, and periods of despondency in childhood and adolescence (Oden, 1980; LeCroy, 1983). Children lacking peer acceptance often are excluded from positive, friendly interactions with peers, and hence a rich source of social learning and practice.

Social skills training interventions have been demonstrated to decrease interpersonal loneliness, improve acceptance and inclusion by peers, and aid in the mainstreaming of handicapped children into regular education settings (Adams, Openshaw, Bennion, Mills, and Noble, 1988; Gresham, 1981).

Learning disabilities and school failure: While social skill deficits are not a causal factor in the presence of a learning handicap, they compound and intensify the difficulties encountered by learning disabled children to a great degree (Cruickshank, Morse, and Johns, 1980; Hendrick, 1988). Learning–disabled children have difficulty interpreting and responding to social cues, discriminating situations, and fitting into social groups. The combination of a chronic learning handicap and social maladjustment can place a youth at risk for involvement in delinquency, school failure, chemical dependency, and serious mental health issues.

Deficits in social functioning appear to be implicated in numerous problem areas confronting children, adolescents, and young adults. The ability to interact effectively with others may be especially critical, though, during adolescence. This is normally a time when a youth would be refining a variety of basic social behaviors and learning more complex skills necessary for the transition to adulthood (LeCroy, 1983). Youth need to become increasingly skilled as they face the developmental tasks of adolescence, such as identity and value formation, independence from family, and appropriate group affiliation. Without a strong social and psychological base from which to develop, many adolescents fail to negotiate these tasks successfully.

▶ Summary

Social skills training programs have repeatedly demonstrated their effectiveness in developing a wide range of interpersonal behaviors and skills in diverse populations of children and adolescents (Kazdin, 1985). The quality of any social skills training effort is enhanced by staff members recognizing the complexity of human social interactions, and choosing a curriculum of skills that will be meaningful and valued by the youth and society. Child–care staff can utilize structured and spontaneous interactions with their youth, both individually and in groups, to build important life–skills and treat behavioral deficits on a daily basis.

CHAPTER TWO

Elements of social behavior

The goal of a social skills training program is to establish in the youth new sets of responses to social situations and teach a youth how to integrate his or her behavior with others in the environment. In order to accomplish this, staff working with the youth must have a clear conception of what constitutes social behavior and social skills, as well as a method of analyzing the youth's current level of functioning. This chapter will focus on the functional relationships between the youth's behavior and the environment, the structure of appropriate social skills and task analysis, and methods of assessing skill deficits and targeting alternative responses.

▶ Functional relationships of behavior

A behavioral approach to social skills training first recognizes that all behaviors occur within a context of environmental events. A youth engages in a particular behavior or activity, in a given situation, in order to have some effect on his or her surroundings. Examples of this may include getting someone's attention, obtaining a possession, or being left alone. But the result of that behavior, whatever the original intent, also will have an effect on the youth. Thus, the relationship between a youth's behavior and the environment is bidirectional or functional. The youth is affecting the social environment, while the environment is simultaneously affecting the youth.

The events in the environment that may serve to modify or control a youth's responses are numerous, but can be generalized into two main categories: antecedent events and consequent events. Both of these are closely associated in time with the occurrence of a behavior.

▶ Antecedent events:

An antecedent event represents the situation or conditions immediately preceding a behavior or performance of a skill. Often, the antecedent event is a cue to a person that a particular behavior would be an appropriate occurrence. For example, a ringing doorbell is a cue or antecedent event for going to the door and answering it.

Antecedent events are critical when attempting to analyze a problem behavior the youth may be demonstrating. The staff may be able to examine the events immediately preceding a negative behavior (such as a tantrum or becoming physically aggressive) and begin to detect patterns in the behavior's occurrence. A youth may, for example, begin to argue and whine when told "No," but not when he or she is asked to complete a chore. In this case, the antecedent event would indicate to the staff that additional time needs to be spent teaching the youth the social skill of "accepting 'No,'" and not as much time on the skill of "following instructions." The pattern of antecedent events that may be revealed around any particular behavior problem or skill deficit of a

youth will help determine the appropriate alternative skill to teach.

It also should be mentioned that improvement in problem behaviors, as well as gains in social skills, can be accomplished through manipulation of antecedent events (Gresham, 1981). If a parent complains that his or her child always loses his or her temper when told to go to bed, observation may reveal that the parent walks into the living room in the middle of a television show each night and commands the child to go to bed. Changing the antecedent event by having the parent prompt the child 15 minutes ahead of time that bedtime is approaching and negotiating a bedtime that is at the conclusion of the youth's television show may be sufficient to prevent the problem from occurring.

Recognition of antecedent events and choosing correct responses can be a major challenge for social skill–deficient youth. Situations that are ambiguous, including vague verbal or nonverbal responses from others, are easily distorted and misinterpreted by youth with social deficits. The misattribution of intent in ambiguous situations has been viewed as a major precursor to aggressive acting out in some youth (Patterson, 1982). Therefore, one area of teaching that should not be ignored by a child–care staff that is attempting to improve their youths' social competency is the recognition of situational cues, and strategies for dealing with these cues when they are confusing or easily misinterpreted.

▶ Consequent events:

Consequent events (or consequences) are the outcomes that result after a particular behavior or skill has occurred. Broadly speaking, behavioral consequences can be classified into two general types: reinforcing and punishing. Reinforcing consequences invariably strengthen the behavior they follow, and negative consequences weaken the behavior they follow.

Consequent events also are critical to analyze when staff are attempting to decrease a problematic behavior or increase a positive behavior. Reinforcement for a negative behavior such as tantrumming may come in the form of parents giving into demands for a possession, or ignoring the child and ceasing interactions with him or her. Both responses may increase the likelihood that, given a similar situation in the future, the child will tantrum again. But remember that the relationship between the child's behavior and the environment is bidirectional. If the parents' giving in or ignoring produced an immediate cessation of the child's tantrum, *they* are more likely to respond in a similar fashion in the future. This, in turn, increases the likelihood of even more tantrumming from their child, which produces more avoidance from the parents, and so on. Such is the nature of functional relationships.

Likewise, when positive behaviors are consistently reinforced in the social environment, they will increase in frequency over time. In order to establish and maintain new social skills in a youth, the child–care staff must reinforce the occurrence of these skills at a high rate, especially at first. When the youth begins to experience the natural reinforcement that results from improved social skills (comfort in social situations, better peer acceptance, more effective communication), the staff's rewarding of those behaviors becomes less important and can be faded out.

In conducting a functional analysis of a youth's social behavior, the child–care staff begins by observing and describing the antecedent and consequent events that appear to precede and follow each significant behavior. Between these two descriptions, a detailed account of the youth's behavior is recorded. By analyzing each component (the **Antecedent —— Behavior —— Consequence**), the staff should obtain a relatively clear picture of: 1) what events appear to be cues for the behavior to occur; 2) the consequences that seem to be maintaining the behavior; and 3) what appropriate social skill should be taught in order to replace the youth's current problem behavior. An example of a functional analysis is provided in Figure 2.1 that follows:

Antecedent event	Behavior	Consequent event
Billy approaches a staff member and asks to go outside and play. The staff person says, "No, it is time to get started on your homework."	Billy begins to argue, raise his voice, curse, and complain that the staff person is never fair to him.	The staff person responds with "OK", you can go outside, but only for 20 minutes." Billy calms down immediately and leaves to go play outside.

Figure 2.1

By analyzing the preceding interaction according to a functional analysis model, we could obtain the following information:

1. The situational cue for Billy beginning to argue and curse appears to be when he is denied a request (or told "No");

2. The consequent event that is likely to maintain the behavior is the staff person giving in to Billy's arguing and complaints about fairness, and that Billy was able to engage in an enjoyable activity immediately following the behavior;

3. The two skill areas apparently in need of improvement in this example are Billy's difficulty accepting "No" answers and his instruction–following behavior.

This example illustrates the information that can be obtained through a functional analysis exercise and observation of a youth's social behavior. The critical elements of any behavior pattern are the events that precede and follow the target behavior or skill, and the specific verbal and nonverbal components of the skill.

▶ Social skill components

In a behavioral teaching program, it is important to distinguish between "skills" and the behaviors that are part of them. Behaviors are individual, discrete, observable acts demonstrated as part of a larger measure of activity. Some behaviors may be so subtle that they are performed unconsciously (such as looking at a person who is talking to you) and may be part of nearly every social skill.

Skills, on the other hand, are sets of related behaviors or components that are designed to produce positive results for the user in defined situations. It is the consistent and generalized use of such skills that constitute "social competency" (LeCroy, 1983). It is critical that a child–care staff become adept at defining, recognizing, teaching, and reinforcing the behavioral elements of social skills.

The elements of social skills are identified and defined through a process called "task analysis" (Cartledge and Milburn, 1980). The essential steps involved in the task analysis of a social skill area are: 1) specifying the desired outcome or goal; 2) identifying the essential component behaviors of the goal or skill; 3) stating the behavioral elements of the skill in observable terms; and 4) sequencing the component behaviors in order of performance. If, for example, a desired outcome for a particular youth was stated as "will comply with directions," the process listed above might instruct staff to teach the youth to: 1) look at the person giving you the instruction; 2) acknowledge that you heard the instruction; 3) get started right away and stay on task; and 4) let the person know when you are done.

It is important when task–analyzing social behavior to remember that the youth is the primary one who needs to comprehend the listing of individual behaviors. Therefore, the analysis of social skills, if it is to be an effective treatment tool and resource, has to be concise, clear, and written in objective terminology. Figure 2.2 summarizes guidelines for effective task analysis of social skills.

Deficits in social functioning can be measured and assessed in numerous ways. The primary methods of formal assessment, mainly in populations of younger children, include sociometric measures, naturalistic

Guidelines for task analysis

1. The scope of the main task or skill should be kept limited.

2. Subtasks (behaviors) should be written in observable terms.

3. Terminology should be at a level understood by the potential user.

4. The task should be written in terms of what the learner will do.

5. The task, not the learner, should be the focus of attention.

(Moyer and Dardig, 1978)

Figure 2.2

observation and recording, and teacher/caregiver ratings (Gresham, 1981; Oden, 1980). These techniques are primarily designed to produce ratings of peer acceptance, popularity, and social integration that can be correlated with other characteristics of children scoring particularly low or high on these measures.

Assessments based on observations of the functional contingencies surrounding problem behaviors are useful for targeting specific skill deficits in a youth (see previous example in Figure 2.1). Once these deficits are observed and defined, the child–care staff chooses appropriate alternative skills to teach as substitutes. This is

Primary skill deficiencies of conduct-disordered youth

Type	Primary skill deficiencies
	1. Self–control/anger management
Aggressive	2. Negotiating
	3. Asking permission
	4. Avoiding interpersonal conflict
	5. Sensitivity to others
	6. Dealing with anger of others
	1. Conversation skills
Withdrawn	2. Dealing with fear and stress
	3 Decision–making/problem–solving
	4. Expressing feelings and apologies
	5. Responding to persuasion
	1. Responses to teasing and failure
Immature	2. Responses to group pressure
	3. Competence in sharing and play
	4. Goal–setting
	5. Task–orientation/concentration

Figure 2.3

accomplished most effectively on an individual, prescriptive basis for each youth. However, some generalities can be made in order to demonstrate how the choice of opposite competing skills is targeted. Goldstein et al., (1980) analyzed the skill–deficiency structure of each major subtype of conduct–disordered youth (Aggressive, Withdrawn, and Immature). Their formulation is summarized in Figure 2.3.

The process of developing skill–based interventions for youth with difficult behavioral problems is initially dependent on the staff's ability to clearly specify and target areas needing remediation. Agreement then needs to be reached regarding what skills constitute "behavioral opposites" and how they will be taught. For example, if one youth accompanies another in a shoplifting episode, and part of the staff is teaching "Honesty" while others are teaching "Resistance to Peer Pressure," chances are the youth will not receive particularly effective help in either area.

▶ **Summary**

The fundamental elements of a youth's social behavior and skills include the context or situational variables in which they occur, the behavioral components that the youth is capable of performing, and the consequent events that affect future performance. Also, in order for the youth to become socially "competent," he or she needs to be capable of recognizing the subtle social cues emitted by others in the course of an interaction and must be able to make appropriate behavioral adjustments.

In the Boys Town Family Home Program, a comprehensive curriculum of social skills is utilized to guide the staff's instructional interactions and treatment planning. This curriculum is presented in Chapter 5. Each skill is task-analyzed and cross-referenced with related skill areas and relevant treatment issues in order to augment the treatment planning process for serious youth issues or special populations.

CHAPTER THREE

Individual teaching techniques

A child or adolescent who is deficient in critical social skill areas may not have had the benefit of growing up in an environment where positive social behavior was taught or reinforced. Appropriate styles of interacting with others may not have been modeled by the adults present or valued by the local peer culture or neighborhood. The child, therefore, may have not received any direct instruction in appropriate ways to get his or her immediate needs fulfilled, as is typical in most functional family settings (Oden, 1980).

The lack of reinforcement for important social skills may be a particularly critical feature in the learning histories of children with serious behavioral and emotional problems. For example, Patterson (1982) and his colleagues found that parents of children who were later described as having aggres-sive behavior problems were more likely to: 1) use harsh commands and demands with their children; 2) reward negative behaviors with attention or compliance; and 3) ignore, or even punish, prosocial behaviors that their children demonstrated at home. These children, then, are more likely to act out aggressively in conflict situations at school and with peers, and to be deficient in critical social skill areas such as compliance with rules, problem–solving strategies, and communication skills. While one task of the child–care treatment provider and educator may be confronting inappropriate behaviors that occur, another simultaneous task is to encourage and motivate the child to replace those behaviors with more socially adaptive responses.

The techniques covered in this chapter are used with children and youth individually to build their repertoire of social skills. Most models of social skills instruction incorporate components such as modeling and demonstration, role–playing, performance feedback, and activities to promote generalization (Goldstein et al., 1980). These techniques, covered in this chapter, are divided into methods of teaching social skills initially in a planned format, and then methods for subsequently reinforcing and/or correcting the child's spontaneous use of these skills.

▶ Specifying behaviors

A key ingredient in any instructional interaction with a child is specificity. This means that behaviors and skills that are being taught are clearly defined and even demonstrated for the child, leaving as little room for potential confusion as possible. Chapter 2 referred to the specific components of appropriate social behavior and task analysis. This same degree of specificity and objectivity must be reflected in the verbal interactions between child–care staff and their youth.

There are numerous advantages of teaching social skills in a clear, concrete manner. The overall effectiveness of a staff member's instructional sequences increases dramatically as the language used becomes more specific and objective. Youth are more likely to learn the components of social skills and, once learned, are more likely to generalize those skills to other situations in which it would be appropriate to use them (school, home, on the job, etc.). This may be particularly critical for those youth with cognitive or learning problems. For example, a learning–disabled child may have particular difficulty understanding vague instructions from teachers or caregivers, recognizing and interpreting the social cues of others, and choosing the appropriate social response in a given situation (Cruickshank et al., 1980). Clear descriptions and demonstrations of behaviors and skills may help these youth learn more efficiently and, subsequently, handle difficult or ambiguous social situations more successfully.

The process of describing skill components specifically and objectively also may enhance the quality of staff–youth relationships and build trust. Many youth in treatment programs or institutions have been told repeatedly what not to do or have been "put down" for the problems they may have. But when staff take the time to instruct youth in a positive, objective manner, focusing on the skills to use in situations that have caused them difficulties in the past, they are communicating care and concern for the youth in a tangible way. As a result, the youth become more open to the staff's teaching and intervention and are more likely to try out the new skills and behaviors they have been taught. This is especially true when child–care staff are careful to avoid judgmental and value–laden terminology that may harm a child's self–esteem or trigger an emotional reaction (such as "that was wrong," "bad," "stupid," or "terrible").

▶ Identifying what skills to teach

The practical application of individual teaching techniques for building social skills begins with the identification of what skills will be taught to a youth. In terms of content and sequencing, individual teaching sessions can focus on: 1) a progression of social skills from basic to more advanced; 2) social skills specifically identified to be relevant to the youth's most critical treatment issues or needs; 3) preparation for a specific set of circumstances or event; or 4) all of the above. An important consideration in this process is that the youth begins to see the value in the skills that are chosen to be taught (LeCroy, 1983). If the youth perceives appropriate social skills as meaningful only to the adults who are teaching them, the likelihood of that youth internalizing and generalizing these skills is greatly diminished. It is therefore critical that the teaching process utilized to train the youth in a new set of social skills includes steps that explain the personal benefits of learning such skills.

For the most part, the choice of which particular skills to teach a youth varies with the youth's current level of functioning, immediate needs, and long–term treatment goals. Once the skills have been identified and prioritized, a staff member can utilize a structured teaching format called Planned Teaching in order to conceptualize and then define a particular skill for the youth.

▶ Planned Teaching interactions

The Planned Teaching format is a method of teaching and demonstrating a new skill for a youth at a neutral time. The term "neutral time," in this sense, refers to time periods during a youth's day when no other activities are occurring, the environment is relatively free of distractions, and the youth is cooperative and not engaging in any overtly inappropriate or noncompliant behaviors. If these behaviors are occurring, Planned Teaching should not be attempted until the youth has regained control of himself or herself and will cooperate. The focus of Planned Teaching is on positive skill–building and augmenting the corrective intervention techniques used by the staff, not substituting for them.

The Planned Teaching Interaction makes use of several concepts of effective teaching at once: praise and reinforcement, specificity, modeling, direct instruction, role–play, etc. These skills are organized into a sequence of verbal statements to the youth that make up the planned instruction in a social skill area. The eight steps of the Planned Teaching Interaction are listed in Figure 3.1.

Planned Teaching components

1. Introduce skill/Give examples

2. Describe/Demonstrate skill components

3. Rationale

4. Request for acknowledgment

5. Practice cue

6. Practice feedback: Praise Describe performance

7. Positive consequence

8. Prompt future practice/Praise

Figure 3.1

Introduce skill/Give examples: The child–care staff or teacher conveys to the youth what they will be discussing and identifies the skill to be learned. The skill area is named and labeled throughout the interaction and several examples are given of situations in which the youth may be called upon to utilize the skill. The relevance of the skill to the youth's own experience is emphasized.

Example: *"Thanks for sitting down to talk with me, Billy. I wanted speak to you today about a skill that may really help you here, and when you leave and go back home. I'm talking about a skill called 'following instructions.'*

You may get instructions from the staff around here, or get instructions from your teachers at school. And when you go home, I'm sure your mom will have instructions she will want you to follow."

Describe/Demonstrate skill components: The staff person breaks the skill down into specific, understandable steps that the youth is capable of performing. Particular attention is paid to nonverbal physical behaviors (facial expressions, voice tone, gestures, and mannerisms), in addition to the verbal responses that the youth should demonstrate.

Example: *"When someone gives you an instruction, Billy, you should look at them, and with a pleasant voice say something like 'OK' or 'Sure.' Then, do the task right away and, when you're done, check back with that person by saying something like 'OK, I'm done. Is there anything else?' That would be how to follow instructions really well!"*

Rationale: The rationale component presents an opportunity for the staff person to explain to the youth how learning the new skill will directly benefit him or her. The focus of the rationale should be personal to the youth, and should relate the skill that is being taught to a goal or desire the youth has for his or her life. Rationales should not be long–winded explanations or lectures, but rather brief and to the point.

Example: *"I know you have been wanting to get a job this summer, Billy, and learning how to follow instructions really well* will be a big part of your getting one and keeping it all summer. I bet then you'll have more money to spend on that new skateboard you've wanted."

Request for acknowledgment: Since the youth's "buying into" the importance of learning new social skills is so critical, the child–care staff will want to quickly assess the youth's understanding of rationales that are given. A specific request for acknowledgment of understanding is made in order to make this assessment, as well as to make the entire interaction more of a dialogue. Requests for the youth's acknowledgment should occur throughout the entire interaction.

Example: *"Billy, does that reason for learning to follow instructions make sense to you?"*

Practice cue: The staff member should have the youth immediately practice the skill so the youth can become comfortable with the component behaviors and so the staff person can assess the clarity of his or her teaching. A role–play or pretend situation should be set up, appropriate to the age and developmental level of the youth, which presents the youth with a realistic opportunity to utilize the new skill. In setting up the practice sequence, the child–care staff should carefully explain what will happen in the situation, and review the skill components again. Practice sessions are particularly effective if they are made to be reinforcing and fun for the youth.

Example: *"I think we should practice following instructions just to make sure you've got it. Let's say I'll be your boss at the restaurant down the street. I'll give*

an instruction and what you will do is look at me, say 'OK' I'll get on that,' pretend to do the task, and then let me know you are done. Do you think we can try that now?"

Staff: *"Billy, I'd like you to carry those boxes back to the storeroom."*

Youth: *"OK, I'll get on that right now."*
"I'm done with the boxes, anything else?"

Practice feedback: When attempting a new skill, the youth is likely to do some of the steps very well and others less so. When providing feedback to the youth on his or her performance, the staff person should encourage the youth by descriptively praising those behaviors performed to criteria and nonjudgmentally describing those that need improvement. After each practice, all feedback should begin with enthusiastic praise and appreciation for the youth's efforts. If the youth is having consistent difficulty with some components, the staff should check to see that the steps are not too difficult, that they were explained clearly, and that the skill is age–appropriate. Skills can be practiced again, but the entire session should not become too lengthy as it can become punishing to both the youth and staff.

Example: *"Nice job, Billy! When I gave you that instruction, you looked at me, used a pleasant voice tone and said 'OK, I'll get on that right now.' Then, you pretended to do the task and checked back with me when you were done. That was a great job of practicing following instructions."*

Positive consequence: It is critical that the youth feels some immediate reinforcement for practicing and learning a new skill. The child–care staff provides some form of tangible reward for the youth's efforts, along with a great deal of social reinforcement and praise. Positive consequences can take the form of privilege–based rewards (TV time, video games, music, etc.) or token–based rewards (points, stars, poker chips, etc.) that can be used later to purchase privileges from a menu.

Example: *"You've really worked hard at this, Billy, and for practicing following instructions you have earned an extra 15 minutes of TV time this afternoon."*

OR

"You really did a nice job this afternoon, Billy. Go ahead and give yourself 500 points for practicing following instructions."

Prompt future practice/Praise: The child–care staff lets the youth know that he or she will be practicing this, and other skills, again in the future. One technique is to follow an initial Planned Teaching session with another role–play within 5 to 15 minutes, and then have several more during the remainder of the day. After each practice, the staff can continue to provide descriptive praise, descriptions of appropriate behaviors, and positive consequences. This will maximize the youth's learning potential during a given time period and help ensure the acquisition of the new skill. The staff person also should end the interaction positively by praising the youth's participation and compliance with requests.

Example: *"Thanks for taking time to go over this skill with me and practicing some new behaviors. It's important that we keep practicing how to follow instructions again so that you can get even more comfortable with that skill. Let's do another practice in about 15 minutes, and you can earn some additional privileges, OK?"*

Planned Teaching, as a format for training youth in new social skill areas, can be utilized to instruct the youth in behaviors needed to successfully negotiate specific problem situations. For example, if a youth is being teased by classmates at school and acts out aggressively (resulting in negative consequences), a specific set of responses to that problem situation can be taught and practiced utilizing the Planned Teaching Interaction.

Social skills training through Planned Teaching serves an important preventive function as well (LeCroy, 1983). Juvenile offenders, in particular, are seen as often relying on inappropriate methods of obtaining reinforcers for lack of any better resources. Individual instruction with these youth may help build a repertoire of skills that, in many circumstances, will preclude the need for deviant social responses. Evidence also exists which suggests that unwanted teenage pregnancy may be reduced with instruction in social skill areas such as problem–solving, sensitivity, appropriate self–disclosure, etc. (Schinke, Gilchrist, and Small, 1979).

Once a skill has been taught to a youth, it is critical that the generalization of that skill be monitored and actively encouraged. Generalization is said to occur when a behavior learned under one set of circumstances occurs, appropriately, under other circumstances (Sulzer–Azaroff and Mayer, 1986). The youth needs to develop proficiency with each social skill the staff teaches, both in the same environment over time and in diverse situations in which the youth may be called upon to function appropriately. However, in the area of social skills training, the issue of generalization and maintenance of teaching is the most elusive and least well–documented (Svec and Bechard, 1988). Techniques for successfully promoting generalization of social skills include: 1) specific techniques utilized within the training process; 2) reinforcement for spontaneous use of appropriate social skills following training; and 3) correction and feedback for inappropriate social behavior following training.

Promoting generalization during training

Several components of the Planned Teaching format are, in themselves, geared to promoting the use of skills across situations. The "rationales" component is likely the most important of these. Well–constructed rationales point out to the youth how learning appropriate styles of interacting with others will produce favorable outcomes in other arenas of his or her life (including school, with peers, at home, etc.). However, for rationales to be truly effective in getting the youth to learn and implement new skills, the staff working with that youth must know his or her individual likes and dislikes, values, and experiences very well.

Knowledge of what a youth finds important and meaningful in life is critical to fostering the internal motivation to change.

Other specific techniques can be utilized during social skills training in order to increase the potential for generalization and maintenance (Sulzer–Azaroff and Mayer, 1986; Cartledge and Milburn, 1980; Goldstein et al., 1980).

Promoting generalization during training

1. Train in different settings

2. Train with different people

3. "Homework" assignments

4. Cognitive mediators: self–talk, imagery and expectation

5. Altering reinforcement contingencies

Figure 3.2

These techniques are outlined as follows:

1. Train in different settings: varying the location of instruction in order to resemble the different situations the youth may encounter. Simultaneously teach the youth to discriminate between situations and successfully identify which skills to use.

2. Train with different people: using more than one staff person to define, model, and role–play the target skills with the youth. It is optimal if persons involved with the youth in other stimulus situations can participate (i.e. the youth's teacher or counselor, a parent, peers, etc.).

3. "Homework" assignments: commonly used in group social skills training or on an outpatient basis. The youth is given an assignment to utilize a skill in a particular situation, record the outcome, and report back to the instructor to process the result.

4. Cognitive mediators: self–talk, imagery, and expectation: techniques that are designed to internalize behavioral changes by utilizing the youth's own language and cognitive processes as mediators. For example, the use of self–instruction has been found to decrease impulsivity and enhance problem–solving in juvenile delinquents (Hains and Hains, 1988).

5. Altering reinforcement contingencies: in order to increase the natural reinforcement for prosocial behavior. Generalization is enhanced when skills that are taught are ones which will be reinforced by parents, teachers, and peers at higher rates than are the youth's maladaptive responses (Howing et al., 1990).

It is apparent that a number of activities within the skill–training session with a child can and should be utilized to promote generalization and maintenance. However, in day–to–day interactions with their youth, child–care staff should be attuned to the opportunities that are present for rewarding prosocial behavior and correcting inappropriate behaviors that occur. These two processes themselves are critical to the generalization of skills that are taught in planned, structured teaching situations.

▶ Promoting generalization through Effective Praise

As stated earlier, the reinforcement of a youth for attempting to use newly learned social skills is crucial. Frequently, environmental support is insufficient to maintain recently established skills, and in some cases, the environment in which a youth lives may actually resist or punish that youth's effort at behavior change (Goldstein et al., 1980). Therefore, staff working with the young person must actively and creatively reinforce the occurrence of prosocial skills in a manner that the youth finds enjoyable and in which the outcome is educational.

A technique for accomplishing this is called Effective Praise. This interaction is designed to provide a verbal format for child–care staff to sincerely and enthusiastically praise improvements in their youth's behavior and deliver a positive consequence. When a youth engages in an appropriate social skill, particularly one that is the alternative response to his or her typical pattern of behavior, the youth's appropriate behavior should be recognized, described back to the youth, and rewarded. In the Boys Town Family Home Program, Effective Praise is an interaction that is comprised of six steps (Figure 3.3).

Effective Praise components

1. Praise and identify skill
2. Description of appropriate behavior
3. Rationale
4. Request for acknowledgment
5. Positive consequence
6. General praise and encouragement

Figure 3.3

The steps of the Effective Praise interaction are defined and delineated as follows:

Praise and identify skill: The child–care staff begins the interaction on a positive, enthusiastic note by praising the youth for his or her appropriate behavior. The behavior is related to a social skill area that is defined for the youth.

Example: *"Sarah, that was great! You did a really good job of following instructions just then."*

Description of appropriate behavior: The child–care staff specifically describes the youth's appropriate verbal and nonverbal behavior. This step would typically begin by identifying the antecedent, or event immediately preceding the behavior, in order to put the youth's behavior in recognizable context.

Example: *"When I asked you to get started on your chore, the first thing you did was look at me and say 'Sure, I'll get on it.' Then, you did your tasks very quickly and let me know when you were done. That's a great job of following instructions."*

Rationale: The staff person provides the youth with a personalized reason to continue to behave appropriately when confronted with this situation again. The rationale should relate to a value or area of interest that is meaningful to the youth.

Example: *"By following instructions right away, you will have more free time to go outside and ride your new bike."*

Request for acknowledgment: The child–care staff asks the youth to acknowledge that he or she understands what is being taught. Acknowledgment requests take the form of questions that are used throughout the interaction and serve to maintain it as a dialogue.

Example: *"Do you understand what I mean, Sarah?"*

Positive consequence: The staff person gives a positive consequence as a reward to the youth for appropriate behavior, and to increase the likelihood that the behavior will continue to occur in similar situations (generalization). The positive consequence may be a privilege–based or token–based reward and should be delivered immediately.

Example: *"For following instructions so well, you earned an extra 10 minutes of phone time tonight."*

OR

For following instructions so well, you can earn 500 positive points on your point card."

General praise and encouragement: The staff member ends the Effective Praise interaction with a general statement of praise or appreciation for the youth and encouragement to continue. All praise should be sincere and enthusiastic.

Example: *"Thanks for all your effort today, Sarah. Keep up the good work!"*

There are numerous benefits for child–care staff to develop proficiency at Effective Praise interactions and use them consistently in reinforcing their youth. Effective Praise is a powerful teaching tool in that most youth readily respond and listen to an adult who takes the time to praise them. It also increases the likelihood that appropriate skill demonstration will continue because a youth receives a tangible reward for implementing what has been previously taught. As a result, the youth's inappropriate behaviors that the prosocial skills were designed to replace begin to decrease as the youth has little need for them.

In addition, consistent use of Effective Praise by staff serves to enhance the self–esteem, confidence, and feeling of competency of the youth. Possibly for the first time, the youth feel capable of accomplishing tasks and can take pride in their work and behavior. Consequently, the child–care staff are viewed by the youth as being more concerned about them and fairer. The belief that the staff person is willing to acknowledge

Benefits of
Effective Praise

1. Powerful teaching tool

2. Increases the likelihood of future positive performance

3. Decreases inappropriate behavior

4. Enhances youth's self–esteem

5. Helps build positive relationships

Figure 3.4

positive behavior and effort is a key element in the development of positive staff–youth relationships.

▶ Promoting generalization through Corrective Teaching

It is unlikely that a youth's problem behaviors would ever be entirely corrected through the sole use of individual Planned Teaching and Effective Praise. Most youth will require continued intervention concerning problem issues, along with training in alternative ways of responding. Teaching social skills simply provides the youth with more options from which to choose when faced with situations involving social interactions with others.

Benefits of Corrective Teaching

1. Helps maintain staff objectivity and fairness

2. Provides tangible help for youth's problems

3. Reinforces teaching in social skills and promotes generalization

4. Helps create and maintain a positive learning environment

Figure 3.5

In the Boys Town Family Home Program, Corrective Teaching (or the teaching done when an inappropriate behavior spontaneously occurs) is accomplished through a structured verbal interaction by staff called the Teaching Interaction. The Teaching Interaction is a method of communicating with a youth about behavior that needs to be changed and replaced by a more appropriate alternative social skill. The Teaching Interaction incorporates several important behavioral and educational skills, including praise and differential reinforcement, specificity, rationales, consequences, and role–play. Staff can communicate with a youth about problem behaviors more objectively because negative behaviors are viewed as learning deficits rather than personal characteristics. This is particularly relevant when child–care staff are confronted with behaviors such as arguing, cursing, threatening, insulting, and even physical aggression. Without appropriate intervention techniques, staff may resort to inappropriate ways of managing problem behaviors, such as ignoring or isolating the youth, arguing with the youth, or verbal and physical counter aggression.

Corrective Teaching Interactions also provide effective, tangible help for a youth's problem behaviors. In past situations, a youth may have only been punished, criticized, or even ignored as a result of engaging in an inappropriate behavior. Corrective Teaching is an active approach to treatment. When a problem behavior occurs, staff view this as an opportunity for directively teaching a more appropriate alternative response. This is done best when the focus of the Corrective Teaching Interaction is an identified social skill that represents an incompatible alternative to the problem behavior. In these circumstances, the inappropriate behavior itself gives the staff a chance to reinforce the Planned Teaching that has been previously done on that skill. Thus, by spontaneously confronting negative behaviors and immediately reviewing skills that have been taught on a planned basis, staff are enhancing the generalization of those skills. Combined with frequent Effective Praise when the youth does demonstrate appropriate social skills, Corrective Teaching rounds out the prevention–reinforcement–correction system and increases the youth's chances for successful family and community life.

Corrective Teaching also is part of a system that emphasizes positive, caring interactions between child–care staff and their youth. There are specific behaviors staff members can engage in that will help create and maintain a positive learning atmosphere for the youth in their programs. These behaviors include frequent smiling, pleasant facial expressions, humor, calm voice tones and affect, and physical gestures and posture that are not confrontational. These behaviors are referred to as the "quality components" of effective teaching. The degree to which child–care staff incorporate these behaviors into their teaching determines, to a large degree, how well a youth will respond to the content of their teaching. Harsh, overly confrontational behaviors from staff do not teach youth appropriate styles of conflict resolution and, in many circumstances, may represent the antecedent conditions for a youth becoming verbally or physically aggressive (Patterson, 1982).

In the Boys Town Family Home Program, Corrective Teaching is accomplished through the nine–step Teaching Interaction, which is outlined in Figure 3.6.

The nine components of the Teaching Interaction are incorporated into each staff person's style and quality components. The goal is to provide staff with a predetermined format for confronting inappropriate youth behaviors in a positive, educational manner. To most effectively and sensitively meet the individual needs of each youth, child–care staff should consistently use the steps of the Teaching Interaction to correct problems in the youth's social skill performance. Examples of the Teaching Interaction components are presented in Figure 3.7.

Teaching Interaction components

1. Initial praise/Empathy

2. Description/Demonstration of inappropriate behavior

3. Consequences: Negative consequence
   Positive correction prompt

4. Description/Demonstration of appropriate behavior or skill

5. Rationale

6. Request for acknowledgment

7. Practice cue

8. Practice feedback: Praise
   Description of behavior
   Positive correction

9. General praise/Encouragement

Figure 3.6

The nine steps of the Teaching Interaction listed above can help a youth learn more appropriate responses to potential problem situations over time. Effective Corrective Teaching occurs in an atmosphere of genuine concern for the youth where there is a thoughtful, individualized approach to skill–building.

Teaching Interaction example

Initial Praise/Empathy	"Mark, thanks for looking at me while we're talking. I know how much you wanted to go to the concert tonight."
Description/Demonstration and of inappropriate behavior or skill	"When I said 'No,' you began to look away argue."
Consequences	"For not accepting 'No,' you've lost your rec room privileges for 30 minutes. You can earn some of that time back by practicing how to accept a 'No' answer."
Description/Demonstration of appropriate behavior	"Whenever someone has to tell you 'No' you should keep looking at them, say something like 'OK, I understand,' and not argue or pout. If you don't understand, you can calmly ask for a reason."
Rationale	"You'll probably be able to go on more activities because people will see you as responsible and able to control your behavior."
Request for acknowledgment	"Do you understand why you need to accept 'No?'"
Practice cue	"OK, Mark, we're going to practice how to accept 'No.' I want you to ask me again about the concert, and when I say 'No' this time I want you to say 'OK, I understand' without arguing."
Practice feedback	"That was great, Mark! This time you kept looking at me, said 'OK, I understand,' and didn't start arguing. Now that's how to accept 'No.' You've earned back 15 minutes of your rec time."
General praise	"Nice job. Keep trying hard and I know you will do well the next time someone has to tell you 'No.'"

Figure 3.7

▶ Summary

Individual techniques for training social skills with children and adolescents can be summarized as a process that incorporates a planned, proactive method of initial instruction with each youth, utilizing sound behavioral and educational principles. In the Boys Town program, this method is called Planned Teaching. Follow–up reinforcement and teaching reward and encourage the youth, thus promoting maintenance, refinement, and generalization of the skills initially taught. In the Boys Town Program, this is accomplished through consistent use of Effective Praise and the Teaching Interaction.

With time, progress, or the emergence of new treatment issues, different skills are identified for youth to learn. The youth learn optimally when all components of the treatment program are applied concurrently and supportively. Individual social skills training represents a crucial part of this program and is an effective method of treating serious behavior deficits in children and youth on an ongoing basis.

CHAPTER FOUR

Social skills training in group settings

Another alternative for teaching interpersonal skills to children and adolescents is utilizing a group teaching format. A group setting provides an immediate social environment in which specific skills can be taught and practiced, and in which a youth can gradually become sensitized to his or her role as a group member. This is an important process because of the numerous "groups" we are called on to function in as a part of normal family and community life (employee groups, political parties, PTAs, etc.).

One hallmark of the Boys Town Family Home Program is a system called "Self-Government," which encourages group participation and decision-making (Father Flanagan's Boys' Home, 1991). One of the components of the Self-Government System is a nightly meeting of the youth and their Family-Teachers called "Family Meeting." Within the structure of this meeting, each youth has an opportunity to discuss problems, offer potential solutions, and even vote on certain house rules. The Family-Teachers use this nightly meeting to encourage group problem-solving, give each youth a chance to give input into the operation of the program, and teach a wide variety of important social skills (discussion skills, giving and receiving criticism, reporting problems, etc.). In this way, each youth's individual treatment program can be augmented by what is learned and reinforced during Family Meeting. Similarly, by incorporating a social skills training group into whatever setting the child is receiving treatment or education, individual goals and target areas can be addressed and skills effectively taught and maintained. In other words, the advantages of a group teaching format can be applied to each youngster's individual benefit. In this chapter, we will review these advantages, some previous uses of group social skills training, a structured format for conducting social skills groups, and techniques for maintaining productive group meetings.

▶ Advantages of group teaching

There are numerous rationales for incorporating social skill-building groups into child-care programs and educational settings in order to augment individual efforts. The group provides a ready-made social setting in which to assess each member's ongoing social functioning under a variety of circumstances, as well as a more naturalistic teaching situation (Trower et al., 1978). The youth's ability to participate in the group activities, concentrate on lessons and tasks, and respond to performance demands may give the child-care staff valuable insight into potential problems in other situations that would require similar skills (such as being in a classroom).

Because social skills training groups allow several youth to participate together, there is increased opportunity for each member to share his or her responses to problem situations, the differing perspectives, and to perhaps generate alternative ways of handling difficult circumstances (Hazel et al., 1983). This may be especially important for those children with learning or cognitive deficits who tend to rigidly stick to one response set in diverse situations. Participation in a group may communicate the message that there are numerous ways to handle stressful or demanding situations and that the youth's previous strategies represent only one option. Many times this message is communicated most effectively by the youth's peers themselves.

There is also evidence that behaviors and skills learned in a group setting may come under control of a greater number of discriminative stimuli, thus increasing the probability that learned skills will be used in situations outside the group (Howing et al., 1990). The effect, therefore, would be greater generalization of the specific social skills taught in the group to diverse situations confronting the youth and maintenance of these skills following treatment. This is especially true when several different training techniques (as well as different trainers) are used to enhance and prompt generalization. And, in addition to the benefits listed above, the provision of social skills training in group settings can increase the number of youth who may be served by a particular program or may increase the cost-effectiveness of a program with limited staff or resources. The advantages of conducting social skills training in group settings are summarized in Figure 4.1.

Advantages of
group settings

1. Assessment of social functioning in group

2. Training in more realistic setting

3. Opportunity to share experiences and options

4. Enhances generalization and maintenance

5. Cost- and time-efficient

Figure 4.1

Group social skills training has been utilized in numerous treatment settings, schools, and outpatient programs. The populations and age groups that have been served using this format have been extremely diverse as well. A group that has received particular attention in regard to social skills training is the one comprised of juvenile delinquents. This is no doubt due to the well-documented relationship between low social skill functioning and delinquent behavior in adolescents and young adults (see Chapter 1).

Several studies have shown the effectiveness of using group teaching techniques with groups of juvenile delinquents. In one report (Shivrattan, 1988), incarcerated male delinquents participated in a social skills training program designed to increase cognitive empathy in participants. The results showed that these youth improved on measures of considerateness, insight, and anger

control. In addition, a one-year follow-up of the participants revealed that they had lower rates of recidivism and better community adjustment than their counterparts in a control group.

Social skills groups also have been conducted with court- adjudicated adolescents on an outpatient basis (Hazel et al., 1983). This typically entails a weekly group meeting lasting 1 1/2 to 2 hours focusing on a limited number of target skills (such as instruction-following, resisting peer pressure, and dealing with interpersonal feedback). In an evaluation of one such program for court-adjudicated youth, Hazel et al. (1983) demonstrated that this effort also produced lower rates of recidivism for group participants after one year than were evident in a comparison group that did not participate in the training.

Social skills training groups have been utilized as part of inpatient psychiatric and day-treatment programs for adolescents as well. For example, conversation skills have been taught to inpatient children and adolescents with the results being better communication behaviors demonstrated both with peers and with unfamiliar adults (Hansen, St. Lawrence, and Christoff, 1989). The effects of an improved style of communication are thought to then enhance the other therapeutic gains made within the psychiatric setting by each individual youth. This also has been considered true for social skills groups conducted as part of day-treatment programming for emotionally disturbed adolescents (Friedman, Quick, Mayo, and Palmer, 1983). In this case, the training resulted in better peer relationships and better conflict resolution within the program, and thus greater gains by the program's participants overall.

Social skills intervention based on a group format has been used effectively in educational settings with both handicapped and nonhandicapped youngsters. In-school social skills instruction has been used with disruptive students in urban high schools to reduce the level of antisocial behavior and discipline referrals (Filipczak, Archer, and Friedman, 1980). An additional benefit of this approach was found to be a corresponding increase in on-task behavior from students and better performance on curriculum measures. The implication of this is that school may, in fact, be the ideal place in which to conduct social skills training groups because the positive effects of training may be more pronounced there anyway. For many young people, school remains the biggest challenge in their lives. By learning new sets of positive, prosocial behaviors within the school environment, students may be more immediately equipped to deal with the academic and social obstacles found there.

▶ Structure and format of the social skills group

In deciding on the structure, scheduling, and content of a social skills training group, a large number of factors must be taken into account. These include issues such as the size and makeup of the group, characteristics of the participants, and decisions regarding who will lead the training exercises. The content of any given session may vary according to the abilities and presenting problems of the youth.

Despite the amount of flexibility that exists in regard to design and implementation of the social skills training program, a few generalities can be made based on previous experience. For example, small groups of 10 or fewer youth are thought to be more effective with regular instruction occurring at least twice a week (Howing et al., 1990). The use of more than one trainer, preferably a male and a female, also has been recommended in order to enhance the potential for generalization and help monitor the behavior of the participants.

The characteristics of the involved children or adolescents are most often determined by the youths' previous grouping or participation in some other primary treatment program. For example, the social skills group may include all of the children in a particular hospital unit or special education class. In these cases, the group members may already know each other or have formed some friendships. Conversely, the group members may be drawn from the population of young people adjudicated by a county juvenile court for a one month period of time. In this case, special activities would need to occur at the outset to introduce group members and make each comfortable with the situation. In both of these examples, however, a positive group atmosphere needs to be created at the outset and maintained by the group leaders. This is critical since the issues under discussion may include alternatives to delinquency or drug behavior, which should not be glamorized or bragged about by group members. Techniques for maintaining a productive training environment will be covered later in this chapter.

Issues related to grouping and participant characteristics also include whether to combine groups of children that are divergent in functioning level or handicap. It is appropriate to combine higher-functioning and lower-functioning children in a social skills training group as long as the behaviors of the higher-functioning children are generally attainable and capable of being modeled and performed by the lower-functioning members (Howing et al., 1990). In fact, the inclusion of nonhandicapped peers into a social skills group for handicapped children is quite positive as the nonhandicapped children's behaviors are more likely to be modeled and imitated, especially if these behaviors result in peer reinforcement (Gresham, 1981).

Prior to beginning the social skills group, the trainers should invest a good deal of time in preparation and planning. The setting should be arranged, materials organized, and reinforcers planned in order to reward positive performance and participation. Additional guidelines for specifically planning instructional content are as follows (Oden, 1980):

1. Select content focus. Select the skill or skills to be covered in that particular session, but limit to probably no more than two.

2. Organize the content. The content and materials should be clearly organized, with particular emphasis on matching the language to be used to the developmental level of the participants.

3. Prepare the oral presentation of material. Plan examples to be used and role-play scenes to be acted out. Prepare answers to divergent responses from group members and how inappropriate behavior will be addressed.

4. Select activities for peer interaction and reinforcement. The social skills instruction may be built around normal activities or a special game. The trainers also should plan reinforcing activities for group members at the conclusion.

▶ Group teaching format

The specific components and format of social skills training are summarized in Figure 4.2. A definition of each component and an example then follow.

Group teaching components

1. Initiation of group

2. Introduction of topic or skill

3. Definition and modeling of the skill

4. Role-play target skill

5. Positive consequence (Individual/Group)

6. Generalization assignment and prompt

Figure 4.2

Initiation of group: The group leaders or child-care staff bring the session to order with a clear beginning prompt or cue that is used consistently to initiate each session. The staff then would welcome the participants and review the expected behaviors from group members and group rules (see Figure 4.3). The group could review the previous lesson or any assignments that were given at the end of the previous lesson. Staff also would prompt the availability of reinforcers or rewards for positive group participation or skill performance.

Example: *"OK, guys, let's bring this meeting to order. [Pause] Good, thanks for quieting down. Before we get started, let's review the rules we established for our group meetings. Tom, can you tell us one?"*

Tom: *"Yeah, we raise our hands before talking and don't just call out."*

"Good, Tom, that's right! Raising our hands will help our meetings be more organized and probably go faster. Does anyone else have a rule they would like to give? If not, then let's see if you have your homework from our last session. Please pass it up front and remember that if you are turning in your assignment, you can earn an extra 15 minutes of game time on the computer. Also, I want to remind you guys that if you work hard on today's skills, you can earn up to a half hour of extra TV time this afternoon. OK, let's get started."

Introduce topic or skill: Here the staff person or group leader introduces the skill or group of skills that will be the focus of the session. They are stated as a concept and labeled by the name that they will be consistently called. Then, the group leader talks about situations that may require the use of the target skill (or first skill to be discussed). Examples of these situations may be first given by the leader but then solicited from the group. This not only promotes more meaningful involvement, but also helps to solicit the ongoing level of understanding of the group members. The leader also may ask the youth how they have handled these types of situations in the past and whether those responses have resulted in negative consequences.

Example: *"We are going to talk today about two skills that will really help you all here in the program and when you go home to your parents. The two skills are 'accepting "No" for an answer' and 'disagreeing appropriately.' The first one has to do with what you might say when you want to do something and the person you ask tells you 'No.' An example might be if you want to go outside, but your Mom says that dinner is almost ready so the answer is 'No.' What are some other times you may be told 'No?'"*

Bill: *"I might ask my teacher if I can get some water and he could tell me 'No.'"*

"That's a good example, Bill. Tell me what you have done when things like that have happened before?"

Bill: *"I guess I usually got pretty mad and lost my temper."*

"OK, and can anybody tell us what could happen if you get mad and lose your temper in school?"

Tom: *"I know when I've gotten mad like that I usually ended up in the office."*

"You're right. That could happen. So today we are going to talk about a different way to handle being told a 'No' answer."

Definition and modeling of the skill: The instructors now verbally and visually define the component behaviors of the target skill. This is first done with a verbal explanation of each step in the response chain. During this time, the responses are being listed on paper or a chalkboard. The instructors then model the use of these behaviors by rehearsing a scene drawn from one of the examples given during the previous step. Modeling scenes can be repeated or several can be done in a row in order to help facilitate the youths' understanding. The group leaders generate (then solicit from youth) rationales for using the appropriate response sets versus inappropriate ones that may result in negative consequences for the youth.

Example: *"Whenever you encounter a 'No' answer, you should do these things: First, continue looking at the person you are talking to. Second, acknowledge the answer by saying something like 'OK' or 'Sure, no problem' in a pleasant tone of voice. Third, don't include any behaviors like whining, arguing, or mumbling under your breath. And fourth, if you have a question, ask the person if you can discuss your request later on. If you do those things, you will be accepting a 'No' answer really well. In fact, to show you guys what we're talking about, Laurie and I will practice this skill here using Bill's example of asking his teacher if he can get some water."*

Note: Instructors Role-Play Target Skill

"Did everyone see what we did here? When I told Laurie 'No' about getting some water, she continued looking at me, said 'OK, maybe later,' and did not argue or whine. The reason these behaviors are so important is that the person who had to tell you 'No' this time may be willing to negotiate later on for something else if you can accept the first answer without arguing or becoming aggressive. Does everybody understand that? Can anyone else think of another reason to accept 'No' answers appropriately?"

Tom: *"Maybe because if you get angry you'll just end up in more trouble than you started with."*

"That's right, Tom, and maybe make the other person angry back at you and less willing to ever say 'Yes' to you when you want to do something in the future. Anyone else have a reason they think we should accept 'No' answers like this?"

Role-play target skill: In this step, each youth is given a chance to behaviorally rehearse the target skill several times in order to learn and begin to generalize the component behaviors. This begins with the instructors reviewing the components of the target skill and then setting up realistic role-play situations, possibly based on examples offered by the youth at the outset of the group. The recommendation is for each youth to practice the skill first with one of the instructors, and then with a peer. The staff follows up each practice with immediate behavioral feedback for the youth by: 1) praising the youth's efforts; 2) describing the parts of the role-play that were correctly done to criteria; and, 3) describing any component behaviors that were left out or not performed to criteria. The emphasis, however, should be on making the practices fun and reinforcing, and avoiding a test-like atmosphere. Role-plays between peers should be monitored closely by staff and feedback should be given on their youths' level of participation and seriousness. The instructors should end the practice sequences with praise to the youth for their efforts and a discussion of what was practiced.

Example: *"OK, then, let's review the steps to accepting 'No for an answer one more time and then we can practice it together. Whenever someone tells you 'No,' you should keep looking at them, acknowledge their answer in a calm voice, and not argue or pout. Tom, how about you practicing once with me, and Bill can practice with Laurie? In this situation, Tom, I'll be your dad and you're going to ask me if you can go out with some friends.*

When I tell you 'No,' I want you to use all of the behaviors we just described. After we practice, you and Bill can try a few situations together."

Note: Instructor And Youth Role-Play Skill

"Tom, that was great! You kept looking at me the whole time we were talking, said 'OK, maybe I can go later,' and did not argue or start whining. That's just how to accept 'No' for an answer. Why don't you and Bill try it?"

Note: Youth Practice Target Skills

"You all did a really super job on this skill. You stayed on task and listened really well. I hope you see how accepting 'No' answers in an appropriate way can help you out in school, on a summer job, and even back home with your parents."

Positive consequence for individual and group performance: At this point, each group member is rewarded for the quality of his or her participation in the social skills group. The positive consequences that are awarded can be either privilege-based or token-based, or a combination that incorporates the system that may be in effect in the youths' treatment program. At the conclusion of the group, a reward, such as a special snack or activity, can be offered to the entire group based on some prearranged contingency agreement. The important aspects of the positive consequence component are that: 1) the rewards are meaningful and valued by the participants; and 2) they are specifically paired with whatever behavior the instructors wish to see again in the future and is considered the priority (i.e. participation and effort versus flawless skill performance). NOTE: If a second skill is to be addressed, it is the instructors' choice whether to save the positive consequences until all of the practice and role-play is completed or provide the consequence after each skill is practiced individually.

Example: *"Each of you did really well today. Bill, you've earned 500 points for practicing accepting 'No' for an answer and 500 points for listening and participating in our group today. Tom, since accepting 'No' is a special target area for you, you've earned 1,000 points for doing so well at the role-play and 500 points for staying on task in our group. Everyone also worked so hard today that we can go get some ice cream down the street when we are done here and play 15 minutes of video games when we get back."*

Generalization assignment and prompt: In the final component of our group teaching model, an assignment may be given to be completed outside of group and reported on at the next session. The generalization assignment is a key ingredient in the transfer of training topics to the youth's other life situations (Goldstein et al., 1980). The assignments themselves can range from written homework reviews of group topics to journal recordings on the success (or lack thereof) encountered in implementing the target skills. The group is then adjourned with more prompts and encouragement for the partici-

pants, and opportunity for privilege or reward use.

Example: *"Your assignment for our next meeting is to record in your notebooks the times people have to tell you 'No' this week and what your response to them was. And if you can, try to write down what their reaction was when you accept 'No' in a positive way, that is, by looking at them, saying 'OK,' and not arguing. I'll be interested to see how this skill, and all of the skills we talk about here, help you all out in situations that have caused you problems in the past. If there isn't anything else, we'll adjourn our meeting and go down the street for that ice cream! Thanks, everybody."*

This sample format for a social skills training group is only limited by the instructors' creativity and the needs of the participants. Variations in terms of role-play activities, audiovisuals, reinforcers, etc., only serve to enrich the process and make it more enjoyable for the youth. Leaders of social skills groups have ranked boredom and inattentiveness as the primary barriers to their groups' smooth functioning (Howing et al., 1990). Boredom can be addressed by varying teaching methods and materials, as well as the reinforcement available, in order to maintain the youths' interest and enthusiasm. Inattentiveness is one of many ongoing behaviors that should be closely monitored during the group session and corrected if necessary. Some techniques for addressing the behavior of group participants are discussed next.

▶ Maintaining a productive group atmosphere

A number of procedures can be employed to help maintain a group environment that is enjoyable, yet productive and goal-directed. This is possible only if group members display certain behaviors while participating that are neither distracting, disruptive, nor apathetic (nonparticipation). However, given that a youth would be referred to the group for lower-than-expected social skill functioning, the staff must assume that the positive behaviors necessary for a perfectly smooth-running group will not occur without a significant amount of preventive and ongoing teaching. Even then, it is quite likely that some youth will become distracted, irritable, or even completely lose emotional control during the group session. Overall, the best approach for staff to use is the one that has been thought out and even rehearsed in advance of the problem. It is necessary, therefore, for the group leaders to define which behaviors will be praised and which will receive Corrective Teaching, and what intervention will occur if a youth needs to be removed from the group. The consequences for positive and negative behaviors should be planned out in advance as well.

Once the list of expected behaviors (or rules) for the group meetings has been generated, along with the corresponding consequences, these behaviors can be preventively taught to each potential group member individually and at the initial session. From then on, each meeting is initiated with a review of the group's rules as a preventive prompt and reminder for each member of his or her responsibility. Visual prompts such as posters, handouts, and 3 x 5 cards also can serve as effective cues for appropriate skill demonstration. The preventive work then is rounded off by reviewing what rewards are available at the conclusion of the group session for individuals who display attentive behaviors and participate in activities.

The staff member leading the social skills group then closely monitors the youths' ongoing behaviors during the group session. This is one of the reasons for having two "co-leaders" for each group session. Should a youth require individual attention or corrective feedback, the progress of the group format is not halted but rather can continue. The instructors should remember, however, that ongoing praise and reinforcement of positive group behaviors is as equally critical as corrective feedback regarding any negative behaviors that occur. This will not only help ensure the continuation of those behaviors, but should enhance the positive atmosphere within the group as well. A partial list of behaviors that may occur in the group setting is presented in Figure 4.3.

In addition to the instructors' ongoing prompting and teaching to the youths' behaviors, numerous other approaches have been utilized to maintain productive social skills groups with children and adolescents. One technique for intervening in serious peer conflicts has been referred to as "fair fighting" (Friedman et al., 1983). When two youth become extremely angry at each other, they are initially separated, each going to talk to a staff member alone. They tell their side of the argument

Positive and negative group behaviors to address

Behaviors to reinforce

1. Raising hands and waiting for acknowledgment

2. Being attentive and remaining on task

3. Volunteering and participating in activities

4. Making positive comments about others

5. Following directions and accepting feedback

Behaviors to correct

1. Calling out or leaving seat without permission

2. Distracting others, fidgeting, or yawning

3. Making negative comments or insulting others

4. Bragging about inappropriate behavior

5. Noncompliance, arguing, and complaining

Figure 4.3

to the staff member they are with and are given instructions to calm down. Both youth are then reunited where they observe the two staff members discuss the problem issue from the youths' perspective and arrive at a resolution. This serves the dual purposes of diffusing the immediate crisis situation and modeling appropriate conflict resolution strategies for the youth.

▶ Summary

Social skills teaching in group settings can be a viable program alternative for many children and youth requiring instruction in interpersonal skills. The group setting functions almost like a "sheltered workshop" for socially deficient youth to practice, learn, and generalize skills that will be critical to their success in almost every arena of life. Group teaching also functions effectively as an adjunct treatment strategy for each youth individually. A youth's specific needs are best addressed through a comprehensive, integrated treatment program that prepares the youth for less-restrictive living or educational alternatives and improves his or her overall social functioning.

CHAPTER FIVE

Social skills and treatment planning

This chapter is comprised of the Boys Town Social Skills Curriculum, which is a catalog of 182 skills for successful interpersonal, emotional, and vocational functioning. The skills are drawn from the vast number of situational variables Boys Town's young people may encounter as they grow and develop toward independence. Each skill has been task–analyzed into its essential behavioral elements that may include: 1) specific verbal responses; 2) nonverbal behaviors that may enhance the child's performance; 3) specific behaviors to avoid; 4) cues for the child to engage in a cognitive activity or self–instruction; and in some cases, 5) subclasses of skills that may be learned separately or as a precursor to a more complex skill. The focus here is to construct a comprehensive treatment tool that is flexible and has many uses across numerous child–care and educational settings. Specific use of the Boys Town Social Skills Curriculum in a treatment planning process for difficult youth problems, as well as application of the Skills Curriculum to referral and diagnostic problems, will be described later.

▶ Structure of the Social Skills Curriculum

The skills contained in this curriculum are organized into four groups—Basic, Intermediate, Advanced, and Complex. They are grouped according to the perceived complexity of performance associated with each particular skill, with the degree of difficulty gradually increasing from the first group to the fourth. The difficulty (or complexity) of a skill may increase due to the number of component behaviors required to perform it or the difficulty of the situations associated with the skill, as well as the specific developmental limitations of the child being taught. Additionally, each skill has been assigned a reference number. The numbers are used to identify and label individual skills in the Social Skills Curriculum, and in two appendices and an index at the end of this book. In the appendices and the index, the page number where a skill and its components can be found is listed.

The nature of many of the component behaviors of the listed skills also changes with increasing complexity. Skills found in the more complex groupings of the curriculum will be more likely to contain cognitive or "metabehavioral" steps. Examples of these include cues to the youth to identify characteristics of the immediate situation, notice the responses of other people involved, monitor his or her own responses and feelings, and instruct himself or herself to engage in certain activities. This added area of learning, along with the specific behavioral responses previously taught by the caretaker, greatly increases the youth's repertoire of skills that can be drawn from in complex, and demanding, situations. The Social Skills Curriculum is structured such that the last group is likely to include skills that have many more of these cognitive–based components steps, whereas the first group could be considered more "basic" behavioral skills. Many youth in treatment programs would typically begin learning the Basic social skills first, and then advance to the more complex skill areas contained in the higher levels. But this may not always be the case. The idea is not that all youth would need to learn the skills from each group in the precise order in which they are categorized, but rather that

skills could be chosen from the curriculum that would match each youth's individual behavioral needs, abilities, and treatment issues. The system of groups simply gives the child–care staff or teacher some measure of relative complexity when prioritizing skills for a youth.

Likewise, when organizing the curriculum for a social skills training group, the instructors would require some measure of cognitive involvement and difficulty in order to appropriately match the curriculum content to the abilities of the participants. The appropriate choice of skills to teach a youth or group is critical to the teaching process and the eventual success of the learner. This is especially true when staff are confronted with particularly difficult or troublesome behaviors from their youth. At Boys Town, direct–care and supervisory staff meet in sessions designed to systematically plan the treatment of individual youth. This process, as applied to the treatment of difficult youth problems and behaviors, is described next.

▶ Treatment planning for difficult youth problems

In all likelihood, everyone working or living with children has his or her own idea and definition of what comprises a "difficult" problem behavior. These behaviors often tax the skills of caretakers, as well as their patience, and can prove annoying or even harmful to those in proximity to the child. A working definition of "difficult youth problems" used at Boys Town includes those problem behaviors that can cause harm to the youth and others, which persist chronically over time, and may eventually lead to negative program departure and other negative consequences for the youth. This definition includes behaviors such as stealing, physical aggression, chronic noncompliance, running away, truancy, sexual acting out and sexual aggression, and drug use—all of which necessitate a systematic approach to treatment planning and target skill selection.

In general terms, staff decide what skills to target for "typical" youth problems or treatment issues by first analyzing the functional relationships existing in the youth's environment that appear to reinforce the problem behaviors (see Chapter 2). It also is critical that the specific situations and antecedent conditions in which the behaviors occur be identified and targeted. Staff then can begin the preventive measures that were discussed in Chapter 3, and systematically begin to teach appropriate alternative response sets (i.e. the individual skills listed in the curriculum). The child–care staff or teacher must be sure, however, that the targeted skills are directly opposite of the problem behavior and will occur under the same situational variables that are associated with the problem behavior being treated.

Oftentimes, however, treatment providers encounter large numbers of negative behaviors from their youth, or particularly serious behaviors that do not seem to respond to typical strategies arrived at through the treatment planning process. In these instances, it is helpful to engage in a systematic analysis of a youth's problem behaviors and the contingencies that appear to be supporting them. A process utilized at Boys Town in the formulation of a "specialized"

Steps to formulating a specialized treatment plan

1. Problem inventory
2. Problem selection
3. Problem specifications
4. Baselining
5. Specification of treatment goals
6. Formulation of treatment strategies
7. Follow–up/Revision
8. Maintenance

Figure 5.1

Treatment Plan for difficult youth problems is summarized in Figure 5.1.

Problem inventory: The child–care staff, therapists, and supervisors begin by generating a list of all relevant problem behaviors being demonstrated by a youth. This is, in essence, a brainstorming session designed to inventory all of the youth's behavioral deficits currently being encountered by staff, teachers, parents, etc. The problem behaviors are listed in no particular order or priority, but only as they are mentioned by staff or supervisors. The process of prioritization begins later. This step also gives staff a chance to discuss any frustrations they are having in working with the youth and deal with any negative emotions they may be experiencing.

Problem selection: In this step, staff begin to discuss and then decide what behaviors listed in the youth's problem inventory appear to be of the greatest immediate concern. Supervisors or therapists may assist in this decision–making process by prompting discussion on issues such as: 1) What problem behavior occurs most often? 2) What behavior relates most closely to several other behaviors that were listed? 3) What behavior causes the most trouble or failure for the youth? 4) What behavior presents the greatest danger to others? 5) What behavior causes the most distress to the adults, family members, or peers who interact with the youth? This step should result in a prioritizing of the problem behaviors that were earlier generated and the selection of one primary behavioral issue to be initially addressed. The choice of what problem behavior to focus on should also be a matter of consensus among the staff working with the youth and any supervisory personnel involved. Problems can be compounded in a youth–care program where staff differ widely on the issue of what behaviors are the most disruptive or difficult to address, and behaviors can be treated most effectively when all staff are consistently responding to them in a well–defined manner.

Problem specification: In this step, the problem behavior that has been chosen by the staff to be addressed is clearly defined and specified. This is necessary in order to facilitate more effective treatment by staff and quicker learning of alternative behaviors by the youth. The process of specifying the problem behavior follows a similar functional analysis model mentioned in Chapter 2. The actual circumstances in which the problem behavior consistently occurs are noted, as well as other variables such as time of day, location, and people who usually are present when the behavior occurs. It also is important to note the social or verbal interactions that take place immediately prior to the youth engaging in the inappropriate behavior. These factors help determine the social skill area in which teaching will take place with the youth.

In addition, the youth's actual verbal and physical problematic behaviors are specified. Whether the youth's voice becomes elevated or sullen, whether his or her verbals are sarcastic or threatening, are all important in defining what the problem responses are. When these problem behaviors are clearly defined, staff will be able to more easily identify the appropriate alternative responses to teach in their place. In addition to specifying what the youth's problem behaviors are, the treatment team should list the typical consequent events that have followed the inappropriate behavior. This would include the consequences that have been used by the staff in the past in their attempts to treat the problem, as well as the social responses of others in proximity to the youth (i.e., attention, ignoring, etc.). This analysis can increase the staff's insights into what contingencies have been supporting the youth's problematic responses.

The problem specification step ends with the identification of the alternative skill to teach the youth in the same situations or circumstances that the problem behavior previously occurred. The skills chosen should be "functional" in that they should empower the youth to handle appropriately the situations that have caused him or her (and the staff) the most problems. The emphasis should be on choosing skills that eventually will be reinforcing to the youth and help meet his or her goals and needs in a socially acceptable manner.

Baselining: It is critical for child–care staff to have some knowledge as to the general frequency of the youth's problem behaviors that have been targeted for treatment. By recording how often a behavior is occurring every day, week, etc., staff will be able to measure the effectiveness of their teaching over time. A "baseline" measurement is the frequency of a particular behavior's occurrence prior to a new intervention being utilized. This measurement can be obtained in both formal and informal ways. A formal baseline measurement would be derived from systematic observation of the youth in various circumstances or from carefully recorded clinical/treatment documentation.

The preciseness of the formal baselining process is admirable, but often unavailable to staff in group homes, shelters, schools, etc. An informal baseline measurement also can be used, taking advantage of the staff person's recall of the frequency of events, location, circumstances, etc. The goal is to obtain a rough, but accurate, measure of how often the problem behavior is currently being demonstrated by the youth to use as a basis of comparison after the teaching strategy has been in place for a period of time. The staff planning the treatment intervention also should estimate the frequency of occurrence of the appropriate replacement skill. This will assist them in evaluating whether their teaching is increasing the youth's demonstration of appropriate behaviors while simultaneously decreasing the negative behavior that was targeted.

Specification of treatment goals: At this point in the treatment–planning process, the child–care staff must decide, given the current level of the youth's functioning, what percent of the time they would initially like to see the youth demonstrate the target skill. For example, the baselining step reveals that a particular youth follows instructions that are given to him or her by staff two out of every 10 times, and refuses to do so eight out of 10 times. Staff might then teach the skill "following instructions" to the youth for the first two weeks with the goal of having him or her improve to five out of 10 instructions followed correctly. Eventually, the goal should be increased to near 90 percent or even 100 percent; however, it is important for both the youth and staff that initial skill demonstration goals be set at reasonable, obtainable levels.

Goal specification also should be related to the components of the particular skill being taught. Thus, the goal of a youth's learning to follow instructions would be that when directed to engage in an activity by the staff, a teacher, parent, etc., the youth will demonstrate all of the component behaviors listed in the Skills Curriculum under the skill "following instructions" (e.g., look at the person, acknowledge the instruction, do the task, and check back). By specifying the behaviors to be demonstrated in those "instruction" situations, the child–care staff working with the youth are more likely to be consistent in their expectations and teaching, thus enabling the youth to be more successful in meeting those expectations and being rewarded for doing so.

Formulation of treatment strategies: In this step of the specialized treatment planning process, the staff agree on what strategies will be used and integrated in the teaching of the target skill (see Chapter 3 "Individual Teaching Techniques"). These strategies may include preventive skill–building exercises and role–play, spontaneous efforts to reinforce positive performance in the skill area (Effective Praise), recognition of negative performance and alternative skill teaching (Corrective Teaching Interaction), and consistent application of rewards and privilege losses contingent on the youth's behavior. Other techniques such as participation in a social skills group, practice with parents or peers, and counseling interventions may be integrated into this plan as well. Also included in this are efforts to promote the youth's generalization of the target skill to other situations and environments that may call for use of the skill. The demonstration of the target skill in other diverse situations is a key indicator of the youth's learning and should be monitored by the staff instructing the youth.

In applying the various teaching strategies, it is important that the staff working with the youth are clear on such issues as how each technique is to be used and applied, when and how often each strategy will be used, and in what situations the staff will use each technique. Again, consistency among the adults working with and caring for the youth is critical. The child–care staff also need a monitoring or data collection system to track the youth's performance in the targeted social skill area. This can take the form of point cards, tally sheets, staff logs, or direct observation records by supervisory staff. The emphasis here is on collecting sufficient information to evaluate the effectiveness of the teaching strategies that were used in order for successful techniques to be continued and less productive techniques to be revised.

Follow–up: Subsequent to the implementation of the skill–based teaching plan, the staff meet to review the treatment goals that were set with the youth and the progress that has been made. Part of this process is comparing the youth's current level of functioning in the targeted skill area with the baseline data that were recorded initially. If negative data trends are detected (i.e. the youth has made no progress or demonstrates the skill less frequently than before), the plan should be reviewed. There may be problems in the implementation of the teaching plan by the program staff that can be corrected with further training or specification of the strategies to be used. Oftentimes, staff need a good deal of encouragement and support to respond differently to a youth's behavior than they previously did. However, if the teaching plan appears to have been implemented correctly and been given sufficient time to take effect, but still produced no progress with the youth, the staff can revise specific aspects of the Treatment Plan, such as the frequency of Preventive Teaching and cued practice exercises, the rewards and consequences that are being offered, or even the skill itself. The important part of this process is that such decisions are made based on concerted observation of the youth's skills and any data that can be collected.

If the data on the youth's learning of the targeted social skill demonstrates a positive trend (i.e. the youth is meeting improvement goals and showing a degree of generalization), staff may decide to continue to use the Treatment Plan as it was initially devised. Added to this, however, would be a higher goal set for performance of the skill, such as the youth following nine or 10 out of 10 instructions that are given to him or her by staff, a teacher, etc. When the goals for this level of performance are consistently being met, a decision can be made to go on the last step of the treatment planning process and focus treatment efforts on other prioritized skill deficits.

Maintenance: The last step of the specialized treatment planning process recognizes that a newly learned skill will not remain in the behavioral repertoire of the youth without the intermittant reinforcement of its use. Thus in this step, the staff devise a specific plan regarding how the youth's progress will be maintained and reinforced. The formal Preventive Teaching and practice sessions may be gradually faded to a point of occurring only once per week or month, compared to daily in the initial plan, and the use of artificial rewards such as privileges may be gradually removed. It is critical, however, that during this fading process, the social reinforcement for the youth's use of the targeted skill be consistent and frequent. In other words, when the youth demonstrates a positive skill that now no longer earns a privilege or point award, the staff should still respond with enthusiastic and meaningful praise for the youth's efforts. The Effective Praise interaction should still be utilized, only without a tangible reward in the consequence step. Follow-up on the youth's progress should be ongoing and can be revised as needed. If a

youth regresses to an earlier level of skill use, the teaching plan utilized earlier (or modifications thereof) can be reinstated by the staff.

The specialized treatment planning process outlined above can be utilized, in various forms, within many different programs and situations involving young people with special needs. The process can be used to address serious behavioral deficits, such as inappropriate sexual acting-out, frequent emotional outbursts, or dishonesty. The process also can be utilized in planning the skill-based instruction of children and youth in numerous other areas as well. For example, the instruction of an older youth in independent living and vocational skills can be systematically planned using a version of this process, as could be the social skill instruction plan for a developmentally or educationally handicapped child.

As an additional aid to the treatment planning process, Appendix A of this manual contains a listing of social skills cross-referenced by behavior problems and Appendix B lists social skill areas cross-referenced by situations. As mentioned earlier, each skill listed in the curriculum is assigned a reference number. Skills are listed by number in Appendices A and B to help staff or caretakers who need to identify skills that may be pertinent to the treatment of a child or youth demonstrating behaviors characteristic of a particular problem area (i.e. aggressive and antisocial behavior, depression and withdrawal, etc.). The skills listed under a particular behavior are those that may positively impact the youth's functioning vis-a-vis that category. Likewise, Appendix B lists several potential problem situations or circumstances a young person may encounter. The skills listed under each problem category are those that may assist the youth in appropriately responding to the demands of that situation. However, in both cases, the decision as to which skills are appropriate to teach a particular youth are individual in nature and must be based on a functional assessment of that youth's needs and abilities. Thus, the charts provided in Appendix A and B are not intended as a "cookbook" for planning the treatment of a given category of a young person, but rather a guide for child–care providers in selecting relevant skills to teach the youth.

▶ Summary

The Boys Town Social Skills Curriculum is an integral part of the child–care and treatment technology developed at Father Flanagan's Boys' Home and utilized throughout the nation. The Boys Town Family Home Program, as a method and philosophy of behavioral treatment, recognizes the need for sound techniques for child–care providers as they confront the challenging needs of their youth and the societal demands placed upon them. Part of this philosophy is the belief that the best preparation for a young person's transition into adulthood can be found in the systematic training of social survival skills for healthy family and community living.

Boys Town's Social Skills Curriculum, combined with positive teaching techniques outlined in this manual, can be an effective tool and guide for child–care providers, teachers, counselors, and parents in their interactions with a youth or several youth. The curriculum also can be utilized in the planning for treatment and intervention with serious youth problems and diagnostic issues, as well as in the preparation of young people for the diverse situations and challenges that lie ahead.

Social Skills Curriculum

▶ **Basic Skills Group**

Skill 1   Following Instructions

Skill 2   Accepting "No" for an Answer

Skill 3   Talking with Others

Skill 4   Introducing Yourself

Skill 5   Accepting Criticism or a Consequence

Skill 6   Disagreeing Appropriately

Skill 7   Showing Respect

Skill 8   Showing Sensitivity to Others

▶ **Intermediate Skills Group**

Skill 9   Accepting Apologies From Others

Skill 10   Accepting Compliments

Skill 11   Accepting Consequences

Skill 12   Accepting Decisions of Authority

Skill 13   Greeting Others

Skill 14   Anger Control Strategies

Skill 15   Answering the Telephone

Skill 16   Appropriate Appearance

Skill 17   Appropriate Voice Tone

Skill 18   Appropriate Word Choice

Skill 19   Asking for Help

Skill 20   Asking Questions

Skill 21   Asking for Clarification

Skill 22   Being on Time (Promptness)

Skill 23   Checking In (or Checking Back)

Skill 24   Completing Homework

Skill 25   Completing Tasks

Skill 26   Complying with Reasonable Requests

Skill 27   Contributing to Discussions (Joining in a Conversation)

Skill 28   Conversation Skills — Initiating

Skill 29   Conversation Skills — Maintaining

Skill 30   Conversation Skills — Closing

Skill 31   Correcting Another Person (or Giving Criticism)

Skill 32   Following Rules

Skill 33   Following Written Instructions

Skill 34   Getting Another Person's Attention

Skill 35   Getting the Teacher's Attention

Skill 36   Giving Compliments

Skill 37   Good Quality of Work

Skill 38   Ignoring Distractions by Others

Skill 39   Interrupting Appropriately

Skill 40   Introducing Others

Skill 41   Listing to Others

Skill 42   Making an Apology

Skill 43   Making a Request (Asking a Favor)

Skill 44   Making a Telephone Call

Skill 45   Offering Assistance or Help

Skill 46   Participating in Activities

Skill 47   Personal Hygiene

Skill 48   Positive Self-Statements

Skill 49   Positive Statements about Others

Skill 50   Refraining from Possessing Contraband or Drugs

Skill 51   Reporting Emergencies

Skill 52   Reporting Other Youths' Behavior (or Peer Reporting)

Skill 53   Resisting Peer Pressure

Skill 54   Saying Good-bye to Guests

Skill 55   Saying "No" Assertively

Skill 56   Seeking Positive Attention

Skill 57   Showing Appreciation

Skill 58   Showing Interest

Skill 59   Staying on Task

Skill 60   Structured Problem-Solving (SODAS)

Skill 61   Table Etiquette

Skill 62   Volunteering

Skill 63   Waiting Your Turn

Skill 64   Willingness to Try New Tasks

▶ Advanced Skills Group

Skill 65   Accepting Help or Assistance

Skill 66   Accepting Defeat or Loss

Skill 67   Accepting Winning Appropriately

Skill 68   Analyzing Social Situations

Skill 69   Analyzing Skills Needed for Different Situations

Skill 70   Analyzing Tasks to Be Completed

Skill 71   Appropriate Clothing Choice

Skill 72   Being Prepared for Class

Skill 73   Borrowing from Others

Skill 74   Care of Others' Property

Skill 75   Care of Own Belongings

Skill 76   Choosing Appropriate Friends

Skill 77   Complying with School Dress Code

Skill 78   Compromising with Others

Skill 79   Communicating Honestly

Skill 80   Concentrating on a Subject or Task

Skill 81   Contributing to Group Activities

Skill 82   Controlling Eating Habits

Skill 83   Controlling Emotions

Skill 84   Controlling Sexually Abusive Impulses toward Others

Skill 85   Controlling the Impulse to Lie

Skill 86   Controlling the Impulse to Steal

Skill 87   Cooperating with Others

Skill 88   Coping with Anger and Aggression from Others

Skill 89   Coping with Change

Skill 90   Coping with Conflict

Skill 91   Coping with Sad Feelings (or Depression)

Skill 92   Dealing with an Accusation

Skill 93   Dealing with Being Left Out

Skill 94   Dealing with Boredom

Skill 95   Dealing with Contradictory Messages

Skill 96   Dealing with Embarrassing Situations

Skill 97   Dealing with Failure

Skill 98   Dealing with Fear

Skill 99   Dealing with Frustration

Skill 100   Dealing with Group Pressure

Skill 101   Dealing with Rejection

Skill 102   Decision-Making

▶ Complex Skills Group

Basic skills for youth

Following instructions
1. Look at the person.
2. Say "Okay."
3. Do what you've been asked right away.
4. Check back.

Accepting "No" for an answer
1. Look at the person.
2. Say "Okay."
3. Stay calm.
4. If you disagree, ask later.

Talking with others

1. Look at the person.
2. Use a pleasant voice.
3. Ask questions.
4. Don't interrupt.

Introducing yourself

1. Look at the person. Smile.
2. Use a pleasant voice.
3. Say "Hi, my name is...."
4. Shake the person's hand.
5. When you leave, say "It was nice to meet you."

Accepting criticism or a consequence

1. Look at the person.
2. Say "Okay."
3. Don't argue.

Disagreeing appropriately

1. Look at the person.
2. Use a pleasant voice.
3. Say "I understand how you feel."
4. Tell why you feel differently.
5. Give a reason.
6. Listen to the other person.

Showing respect

1. Obey a request to stop a negative behavior.

2. Refrain from teasing, threatening, or making fun of others.

3. Allow others to have their privacy.

4. Obtain permission before using another person's property.

5. Do not damage or vandalize public property.

6. Refrain from conning or persuading others into breaking rules.

7. Avoid acting obnoxiously in public.

8. Dress appropriately when in public.

Showing sensitivity to others

1. Express interest and concern for others, especially when they are having troubles.

2. Recognize that disabled people deserve the same respect as anyone else.

3. Apologize or make amends for hurting someone's feelings or causing harm.

4. Recognize that people of different races, religions, and backgrounds deserve to be treated the same way as you would expect to be treated.

Following instructions

Step 1. Look at the person.

Rationale:

Looking at the person shows that you are paying attention.

Helpful hints:

- Look at the person as you would a friend.
- Don't stare, make faces, or roll your eyes.
- Look at the person throughout your conversation. Avoid being distracted.
- Looking at the person will help you understand his or her mood.

Step 2. Say "Okay."

Rationale:

Saying "Okay" lets the person know you understand.

Helpful hints:

- Answer right away.
- Use a pleasant voice.
- Speak clearly.
- Smile and nod your head (if it is appropriate to do so).

Step 3. Do what you've been asked right away.

Rationale:

You are more likely to remember exactly what you're supposed to do if you do it right away.

Helpful hints:

- Complete each step of the task.
- Stay on task. Don't let other things interfere.
- Do the best job you can.
- If you have problems, ask for help.

Step 4. Check back.

Rationale:

Checking back lets the person know that you have followed the instruction.

Helpful hints:

- Tell the person you have finished as soon as you are done.
- Explain exactly what you did.
- Ask if the job was done correctly.
- Correct anything that needs to be done over.

Accepting "No" for an answer

Step 1. Look at the person.

Rationale:

Looking at the person shows that you are paying attention.

Helpful hints:

• Don't stare or make faces.

• Don't look away.

• If you are upset, control your emotions. Try to relax and stay calm.

• Listening carefully will help you understand what the other person is saying.

Step 2. Say "Okay."

Rationale:

Saying "Okay" lets the other person know that you understand.

Helpful hints:

• Answer right away.

• Speak clearly. Don't mumble.

• Don't sound angry or start to argue. That might lead to problems.

• Take a deep breath if you feel upset.

Step 3. Stay calm.

<u>Rationale:</u>

Staying calm allows you to hear exactly what the other person is saying.

<u>Helpful</u> <u>hints:</u>

- If you react negatively, you may make the situation worse.

- People will think you are serious about improving if you stay calm.

- Staying calm shows that you have control of your emotions.

- Accepting a "No" answer this time may improve the chances of getting a "Yes" answer later on.

Step 4. If you disagree, ask later.

<u>Rationale:</u>

If you disagree right away, you will appear to be arguing.

<u>Helpful</u> <u>hints:</u>

- Take some time to plan how you are going to approach the person who told you "No."

- Plan in advance what you are going to say.

- Accept the answer, even if it is still "No."

- Be sure to thank the person for listening.

Talking with others

Step 1. Look at the person.

Rationale:

Looking at the person shows that you are paying attention and shows the person that you want to talk.

Helpful hints:

- Look at the person as you would a friend.

- Look at the person's face; this will help you understand that person's mood.

Step 2. Use a pleasant voice.

Rationale:

People won't want to talk to someone who seems unpleasant, angry, or threatening.

Helpful hints:

- Speak clearly.

- Use short sentences that are easily understood.

- Think before you speak.

Step 3. Ask questions.

Rationale:

Asking questions includes the other person in the conversation.

Helpful hints:

- Avoid asking questions that can be answered with a "Yes" or a "No."

- Ask the person about his or her opinions, likes and dislikes, and interests.

- Listen intently.

- Be prepared to answer questions the person might ask you.

Step 4. Don't interrupt.

Rationale:

Interrupting shows you don't care what the other person is saying.

Helpful hints:

- Make sure the person is done speaking before you respond.

- Maintain eye contact.

- Maintain good posture; don't distract the other person by fidgeting.

- Don't monopolize the conversation or jump from topic to topic.

Introducing yourself

Step 1. Look at the person.

Rationale:

Looking at the person is one way of showing that you really want to meet him or her.

Helpful hints:

• Get the person's attention appropriately.

• Don't stare or make faces.

• Look at the person as you would a friend.

• Looking at the person sets a friendly tone for the beginning of your conversation.

Step 2. Use a pleasant voice.

Rationale:

You will make a good impression if you appear to be friendly.

Helpful hints:

• Speak clearly.

• Talk loud enough to be heard, but not too loud.

• Use proper grammar and avoid slang words.

• Don't interrupt.

Step 3. Offer a greeting. Say "Hi, my name is...."

<u>Rationale:</u>

Saying "Hi" shows you are friendly and makes the other person feel welcome.

<u>Helpful</u> <u>hints:</u>

• Make sure the person hears you.

• Listen if the other person says anything in return.

• Smile if it is appropriate to do so.

Step 4. Shake the person's hand.

<u>Rationale:</u>

Shaking hands is a traditional way of greeting someone.

<u>Helpful</u> <u>hints:</u>

• Use a firm grip, but don't squeeze too hard.

• Three shakes is about right when shaking hands.

• Say "It's nice to meet you" as you shake hands.

• Make sure your hand is clean before shaking hands with someone.

Step 5. When you leave, say "It was nice to meet you."

<u>Rationale:</u>

Saying something nice ends your conversation on a friendly note.

<u>Helpful</u> <u>hints:</u>

• Be sincere.

• Use the person's name again when saying good-bye.

• Remember the person's name should you meet again.

Accepting criticism or a consequence

Step 1. Look at the person.

Rationale:

Looking at the person shows that you are paying attention.

Helpful hints:

• Don't stare or make faces.

• Look at the person throughout the conversation. Don't look away.

• Listen carefully and try not to be distracted.

• Paying attention shows courtesy; looking away shows disinterest.

Step 2. Say "Okay."

Rationale:

Saying "Okay" shows that you understand what the other person is saying.

Helpful hints:

• Nodding your head also shows that you understand.

• Don't mumble.

• By nodding your head or saying "Okay" frequently throughout a long conversation, you let the speaker know that you are still listening carefully.

• Use a pleasant tone of voice. Don't be sarcastic.

Step 3. Don't argue.

Rationale:

Accepting criticism without arguing shows that you are mature.

Helpful hints:

• Stay calm.

• Try to learn from what the person is saying so you can do a better job next time.

• Remember that the person who is giving you criticism is only trying to help.

• If you disagree, wait until later to discuss the matter.

Disagreeing appropriately

Step 1. Look at the person.

Rationale:

Looking at the person shows that you are paying attention.

Helpful hints:

- Don't stare or make faces.
- Keep looking at the person throughout your conversation.
- Be pleasant and smile.
- Look at the person as you would a friend.

Step 2. Use a pleasant voice.

Rationale:

The person is more likely to listen to you if you use a pleasant voice.

Helpful hints:

- Speak slowly and clearly. Don't mumble.
- Use short sentences. They are easily understood.
- Keep a comfortable distance between you and the other person while you are talking.
- Smile. People are more comfortable talking with someone who is friendly.

Step 3. Say "I understand how you feel."

<u>Rationale:</u>

Saying you understand gets the conversation off to a positive start.

<u>Helpful hints:</u>

- Plan what you are going to say before you start to speak.

- If you still feel uneasy about how you are going to start your conversation, practice.

- Start to discuss your concerns as part of a conversation, not a confrontation.

- Be sincere.

Step 4. Tell why you feel differently.

<u>Rationale:</u>

Using vague words can lead to confusion and doesn't get your point across.

<u>Helpful hints:</u>

- Use as much detailed information as possible.

- Be prepared to back up what you say.

- If necessary, practice what you are going to say.

- Always remember to think before you speak.

Step 5. Give a reason.

Rationale:

Your disagreement will carry more weight if you give a valid reason.

Helpful hints:

- Be sure that your reasons make sense.
- Support your reasons with facts and details.
- One or two reasons are usually enough.
- Remember to stay calm during the conversation.

Step 6. Listen to the other person.

Rationale:

Listening shows you respect what the other person has to say.

Helpful hints:

- Don't look away or make faces while the other person is talking.
- Don't interrupt.
- Stay calm.
- Don't argue.

Showing respect

Step 1. Obey a request to stop a negative behavior.

Rationale:

When you obey a request to stop a negative behavior, you show that you can follow instructions. Being able to follow instructions is one form of showing respect.

Helpful hints:

* By stopping your negative behavior, you may avoid getting into trouble.

* There will always be people who have authority over you. You must do what they say.

Step 2. Refrain from teasing, threatening, or making fun of others.

Rationale:

By refraining from such behaviors, it shows you understand that teasing, threatening, and making fun can be hurtful to others.

Helpful hints:

* If you are always making fun of people or threatening them, you won't have many friends.

* People will think of you only as a tease, not as a nice person.

Step 3. Allow others to have their privacy.

Rationale:

Sometimes people need or want to be alone. You show respect by adhering to their wishes.

Helpful hints:

- Always knock before entering someone's room or a room with a closed door.

- Honor someone's desire to be left alone.

Step 4. Obtain permission before using another person's property.

Rationale:

You have certain possessions that are very important to you. You don't want people using them without permission. When you ask permission to use others' things, you show that same kind of respect.

Helpful hints:

- Always return items in the same condition as when you borrowed them.

- If you damage a borrowed item, offer to repair or replace it.

Step 5. Do not damage or vandalize public property.

Rationale:

Vandalism and damaging property are against the law. Besides getting into trouble, you show disrespect for your community and country when you vandalize public property.

Helpful hints:

- Accidents do happen, but they always should be reported.

- Offer to replace or repair property you have damaged.

Step 6. Refrain from conning or persuading others into breaking rules.

Rationale:

People will think less of you if you are always trying to take advantage of others or get them into trouble.

Helpful hints:

- If you use people, they won't trust you.
- People don't appreciate being manipulated.

Step 7. Avoid acting obnoxiously in public.

Rationale:

You make a good impression with people when you show that you know how to behave and use proper social skills in public.

Helpful hints:

- Be on your best behavior in public. That means don't do such things as curse, swear, spit, or belch.
- Be courteous to others and mind your manners.

Step 8. Dress appropriately when in public.

Rationale:

When in public, people are expected to look their best. When you live up to this expectation, you show that you are mature and understand society's rules.

Helpful hints:

- Being well-groomed and well-dressed makes a good impression.
- Use good judgment when deciding what to wear. Where you are going usually dictates what you wear.

Showing sensitivity to others

Step 1. Express interest and concern for others, especially when they are having troubles.

Rationale:

If you help others, they are more likely to help you.

Helpful hints:

- If you see someone in trouble, ask if you can help.

- Sometimes, just showing you care is enough to help a person get through a difficult time.

Step 2. Recognize that disabled people deserve the same respect as anyone else.

Rationale:

A disability does not make a person inferior. Helping people with disabilities without ridiculing or patronizing them shows that you believe all people are equal, although some people need a little extra assistance.

Helpful hints:

- Be ready to help a disabled person when needed by doing such things as holding open a door, carrying a package, giving up your seat.

- Don't stare at disabled people or make comments about their special needs.

Step 3. Apologize or make amends for hurting someone's feelings or causing harm.

Rationale:

Saying you're sorry shows that you can take responsibility for your actions and can admit when you've done something wrong.

Helpful hints:

- You can harm someone by what you fail to do, just as easily as what you do. Some examples are breaking a promise or not sticking up for someone who is being picked on.

- If you hurt someone, apologize immediately and sincerely.

Step 4. Recognize that people of different races, religions, and backgrounds deserve to be treated the same way as you would expect to be treated.

Rationale:

Treating others equally shows that although people are different, you believe that it shouldn't matter in the way you treat them.

Helpful hints:

- Don't make jokes and rude comments about the color of someone's skin or what he or she believes.

- Some people have different customs for doing things. Some people have more money than others. No matter, all people should be treated the same.

Accepting apologies from others

 **Look at the person who is apologizing.**

 Listen to what he or she is saying.

 Remain calm. Refrain from any sarcastic statements.

 Thank the person for the apology; say "Thanks for saying 'I'm sorry'" or "That's OK."

Accepting compliments

 Look at the person who is complimenting you.

 Use a pleasant tone of voice.

 Thank the person sincerely for the compliment. Say "Thanks for noticing" or "I appreciate that."

 Avoid looking away, mumbling, or denying the compliment.

Accepting consequences

 Look at the person.

 Say "OK."

 Don't argue.

 If given instructions or suggestions on how to correct the situation, follow them.

Accepting decisions of authority

 **Look at the person.**

 Remain calm and monitor your feelings and behavior.

 **Use a pleasant or neutral tone of voice.**

 Acknowledge the decision by saying "OK" or "Yes, I understand."

 Possibly disagree at a later time.

 Refrain from arguing, pouting, or becoming angry.

Greeting others

 Look at the person.

 Use a pleasant voice.

 Say "Hi" or "Hello."

Anger control strategies

 If a person is talking to you, continue listening and acknowledging what he or she is saying.

 Monitor your body's feelings and how quickly you are breathing.

 Breathe slowly and deeply.

 Give yourself instructions to continue breathing deeply and relax your tense body areas.

 If appropriate, calmly ask the other person for a few minutes to be by yourself.

 While you are alone, continue to monitor your feelings and instruct yourself to relax.

Answering the telephone

Pick up the phone promptly.

Use a calm, pleasant voice.

Answer the phone by saying "Hello" or "Hello, this is the residence of. . ."

Listen carefully to the other person.

Find the person the caller wants to speak with or offer to take a message.

Write the message down and ensure that the right person receives it.

 End your conversation by saying "Good-bye" or "Thanks for calling," and gently hanging up the phone.

Appropriate appearance

 Use appropriate daily hygiene skills.

 Comb your hair.

Choose clean clothing that will match your day's activities.

 Use a moderate amount of make-up, perfume, or cologne.

 Ask for advice if you are unsure what is proper.

 Maintain your appearance throughout the day (hair combed, shirt tucked in, etc.).

Appropriate voice tone

Look at the person you are talking to.

Listen to the level and quality of the voice tone you are speaking with.

Lower your voice (if necessary) so that it isn't too loud or harsh.

Speak slowly. Think about what you want to say.

Concentrate on making your voice sound calm, neutral, or even pleasant and happy.

Avoid shouting, whining, or begging.

Appropriate word choice

 Decide what thought you want to put into words and then say them.

 Look at the situation and the people around you.

 Know the meanings of words you are about to say.

 Refrain from using words that will be offensive to people around you or that they will not understand.

 Avoid using slang, profanity, or words that could have a sexual meaning.

Asking for help

 Look at the person.

 Ask the person if he or she has time to help you (now or later).

 Clearly describe the problem or what kind of help you need.

 Thank the person for helping you.

Asking questions

Appropriately get the other person's attention without interrupting. Wait to be acknowledged.

Look at the person.

Use a pleasant tone of voice.

Phrase what you are asking as a question by using words such as "Please," "Would," "What," or "May I...."

Listen to the person's answer.

Thank the person for his or her time.

Asking for clarification

Look at the person.

Ask if he or she has time to talk. Don't interrupt.

Use a pleasant or neutral tone of voice.

Specifically state what you were confused about. Begin with "I was wondering if..." or "Could I ask about...."

Listen to the other person's reply and acknowledge the answer.

Thank the person for his or her time.

Being on time (Promptness)

 Know exactly when you need to be where you are going, and how long it will take you to get there.

 Leave with plenty of time to spare (usually about 5-10 minutes before you would have to leave).

 Go directly there with no diversions.

 When you arrive, check in with someone in authority or whom you are meeting.

 If you are late, apologize sincerely for not being on time.

Checking in (or Checking back)

 Promptly return or complete the task.

 Immediately find the appropriate person to check with.

 **Check in by pleasantly saying "Here I am..." or "I'm back from...."**

 **Truthfully answer any questions about your activities or where you have been.**

 End by saying "Is there anything else?"

Completing homework

 Find out at school what the day's homework is for each subject.

 Remember to bring home necessary books or materials in order to complete your assignments.

 Get started on homework promptly, or at the designated time.

 Complete all assignments accurately and neatly.

Carefully store completed homework until the next school day.

Completing tasks

 **Listen carefully to instructions or directions for tasks.**

 Assemble the necessary tools or materials needed for the task.

 Begin working carefully and neatly.

 Remain focused on the task until it is completed.

 Examine the product of your work to make sure it is complete.

 Check back with the person assigning the task.

Complying with reasonable requests

 Look at the person making the request.

 Use a pleasant or neutral tone of voice.

 Acknowledge the request by saying "OK" or "Sure."

 Promptly complete the activity requested.

 If you are unable to do so, politely tell the person that you cannot do as he or she requests.

Contributing to discussions (Joining in a conversation)

 Look at the people who are talking.

 Wait for a point when no one else is talking.

 Make a short, appropriate comment that relates to the topic being discussed.

 Choose words that will not be offensive or confusing to others.

Give other people a chance to participate.

Conversation skills — Initiating

 Look at the person or people you are talking with.

 Wait until no one else is talking about another topic.

 Use a calm, pleasant voice tone.

 Ask a question of the other person or begin talking about a new conversation topic.

 Make sure new conversation topics are about appropriate activities and will not be offensive to other people.

Conversation skills — Maintaining

Continue looking at whomever is speaking.

Maintain a relaxed, but attentive, posture. Nod your head to give ongoing acknowledgment.

Ask follow-up questions that pertain to what the other person just said and show attentiveness.

Avoid fidgeting, looking away, or yawning.

Don't interrupt the other person. If interruptions occur, say "Excuse me" and let the other person speak.

Tell your own stories that pertain to the current topic, but be careful not to dominate the conversation or exaggerate.

Conversation skills — Closing

 Change topics only when everyone appears to be done talking about a particular issue.

 Change to a conversation topic that somehow relates to the previous one, if possible.

 Allow everyone present a chance to talk about the current topic.

 If it is time to depart or move to another area, wait for a comfortable break in the conversation.

 Stand and say "Excuse me..." or "It was very nice talking to you...."

Correcting another person (or Giving criticism)

 Look at the person.

 Remain calm and use a pleasant voice tone.

 **Begin with a positive statement, some praise, or by saying "I understand...."**

 **Be specific about the behaviors you are criticizing.**

 Offer a rationale for why this is a problem.

Listen to the other person's explanation. Avoid any sarcasm, name-calling, or "put-down" statements.

Following rules

 Learn what rules apply to the current situation.

 Adjust your behavior so that you are following those rules exactly.

 Don't "bend" rules, even just a little.

 If you have questions, find the appropriate adult to ask about the rules in question.

Following written instructions

 Read the written instructions for the task one time completely.

 Do what each instruction tells you to in the exact order in which it is written.

 Don't change written instructions or skip any without permission.

 If you have any questions, find the appropriate adult to ask about the instructions in question.

Getting another person's attention

 Wait until the other person is finished speaking or is available to you.

 Look at the other person.

 Get that person's attention by saying "Excuse me...."

 Wait until he or she acknowledges you. Proceed with what you wanted to say.

Getting the teacher's attention

 Look at the teacher.

 Raise your hand calmly.

 Wait to be acknowledged by the teacher.

 Ask questions or make requests in a calm voice.

Giving compliments

Look at the person you are complimenting.

Speak with a clear, enthusiastic voice.

Praise the person's activity or project specifically. Tell him or her exactly what you like about it.

Use words such as "That's great," "Wonderful," or "That was awesome."

Give the other person time to respond to your compliment.

Good quality of work

Find out exact expectations or instructions for tasks.

Assemble necessary tools or materials.

Carefully begin working. Focus attention on your task.

Continue working until your task is completed or criteria are met.

Examine the results of your work to make sure it was done correctly.

Correct any deficiencies, if necessary. Perhaps, check back with the person who assigned your task.

Ignoring distractions by others

Try not to look at people who are being distracting.

Stay focused on your work or task.

Do not respond to questions, teasing, or giggling.

If necessary, report this behavior to a nearby adult or authority figure.

Interrupting appropriately

 If you must interrupt a person's conversation or phone call, stand where you can be seen.

 Wait for that person to acknowledge you or signal for you to come back later.

 When it's time for you to speak, begin with "Excuse me for interrupting, but...."

 Be specific and to the point with your request or information.

 Thank the person for his or her time.

Introducing others

 Position yourself near or between the people you are introducing.

 Use a clear, enthusiastic voice tone.

 Introduce two people by saying each person's first and last names. For example, say "Bill, I'd like you to meet Jeff Thompson. Jeff, this is Bill Smith."

 Allow time for each person to shake hands, greet each other, etc.

 You also may provide more information about each person to the other (their jobs, schools, where they are from, etc.).

Listening to others

 Look at the person who is talking.

 Sit or stand quietly; avoid fidgeting, yawning, or giggling.

 Wait until the person is through before you speak.

 Show that you understand ("OK," "Thanks," or "I see").

Making an apology

 Look at the person.

 Use a serious, sincere voice tone, but don't pout.

 Begin by saying "I wanted to apologize for..." or "I'm sorry for...."

 Do not make excuses or give rationalizations.

Sincerely say you will try not to repeat the same behavior in the future.

 Offer to compensate or pay restitution.

 Thank the other person for listening.

Making a request (Asking a favor)

Look at the person.

Use a clear, pleasant voice tone.

Make your request in the form of a question by saying "Would you..." and "Please...."

If your request is granted, remember to say "Thank you."

If your request is denied, remember to accept "No" for an answer.

Making a telephone call

Accurately identify the number you need to call.

Dial the number carefully.

Ask to speak to the person you are calling by saying "May I please speak to...."

Use appropriate language over the phone; no obscenities or sexually oriented words.

If the person you are calling is not there, ask the person answering if he or she will take a message.

Thank the person for his or her time.

Offering assistance or help

 Ask the other person if he or she needs help.

 Listen to what the person needs.

 Offer to help in ways which you can.

 Do what you agree to do for that person.

Participating in activities

 Appropriately request to be a part of an activity.

 Cooperate with others in the group, such as allowing others to take their turns.

 Use a pleasant voice when talking to others.

 Remember to accept losing or winning appropriately.

Personal hygiene

 Bathe or shower daily.

 Brush your teeth in the morning and at bedtime.

 Brush or comb your hair.

 Put on clean clothes daily.

 **Wash your hands before meals and after using the bathroom.**

 Put dirty clothes in the hamper.

Positive self-statements

 Make positive statements about actual accomplishments.

 Don't lie or exaggerate.

 Begin by saying in a pleasant tone of voice "I'm proud of..." or "I think I did well at...."

 Don't brag or put down other people's efforts.

Positive statements about others

 Try to notice or find out positive things or events about others.

 Use a clear, enthusiastic tone of voice.

 Praise a specific trait or ability of the other person, or congratulate him or her on a recent accomplishment.

 Don't say anything that would invalidate your compliment, such as "It's about time...."

Refraining from possessing contraband or drugs

 Refuse to accept drugs or contraband from strangers or peers.

 Examine your own possessions and decide whether they are appropriate to have (legally, morally, rightfully yours).

 Turn in drugs or contraband to the appropriate adult or authority figure.

 Self-report your involvement. Peer report, if necessary.

 Honestly answer any questions that are asked.

Reporting emergencies

 Identify exactly what the emergency is.

 Immediately find a responsible adult or police officer, or call 911.

 State specifically who and where you are.

Specifically describe the emergency situation.

Reporting other youths' behavior (or Peer reporting)

Find the appropriate adult or authority figure.

Look at the person.

Use a clear, concerned voice tone.

State specifically the inappropriate behavior you are reporting.

Give a reason for the report that denotes concern for your peer.

Truthfully answer any questions that are asked of you.

Resisting peer pressure

 Look at the person.

 Use a calm, assertive voice tone.

 State clearly that you do not want to engage in the inappropriate activity.

 Suggest an alternative activity. Give a reason.

 If the person persists, continue to say "No."

 Ask the peer to leave or remove yourself from the situation.

Saying good-bye to guests

 Stand up and accompany guests to the door.

 Look at the person.

 **Use a pleasant voice tone.**

Extend your hand and shake hands firmly.

 **Say "Good-bye, thank you for visiting" or "Good-bye _____ , it was nice to meet you."**

 Ask the guests to return in the future.

Saying "No" assertively

 Look at the person.

 Use a clear, firm voice tone.

 Say "No, I don't want...."

 Request that the person leave you alone.

 Remain calm, but serious.

 Possibly remove yourself from the situation.

Seeking positive attention

 Wait until the adult or authority figure has time to attend to you.

 Look at the person.

 Wait for acknowledgment.

 Appropriately ask for time to talk.

 Discuss positive events or activities.

 Do not seek attention by whining, pouting, or begging.

Showing appreciation

 Look at the person.

 Use a pleasant, sincere voice tone.

 Say "Thank you for..." and specifically describe what the person did that you appreciate.

 Possibly give a reason it was so beneficial.

 Offer future help or favors on your part.

Showing interest

 Look at the person who is talking.

 Give quiet acknowledgments, such as nodding your head or saying "Uh huh."

 Acknowledge specifically by saying "That's interesting...."

Ask follow-up questions for more information.

Staying on task

Look at your task or assignment.

Think about the steps needed to complete the task.

Focus all of your attention on your task.

Only stop working on your task with permission of the nearby adult who gave you the task.

Ignore distractions and interruptions by others.

Structured problem-solving (SODAS)

 Define the problem Situation.

 Generate two or more Options.

 Look at each option's potential Disadvantages.

Look at each option's potential Advantages.

 Decide on the best Solution.

Table etiquette

 Sit quietly at the table with your hands in your lap.

 Place your napkin in your lap.

 Offer food and beverages to guests first.

 When requesting food, remember to say "Please" and "Thank you."

 Engage in appropriate mealtime conversation topics.

Avoid belching, taking large bites of food, or grabbing your food with your fingers.

When finished eating, ask permission to be excused and offer to clear your guests' plates.

Volunteering

 Look at the person.

 Use a clear, enthusiastic voice tone.

 Ask to volunteer for a specific activity or task.

Thank the person and check back when the task is completed.

Waiting your turn

 Sit or stand quietly.

 Keep your arms and legs still. No fidgeting.

 Avoid sighing, whining, or begging.

 Engage in the activity when directed to do so by an adult.

 Thank the person who gives you a turn.

Willingness to try new tasks

 Identify a new task or activity you've never done before.

 Request permission from the appropriate person.

 Think of all the steps needed for the new task.

 Breathe deeply and try your best.

 Ask for help, advice, or feedback if the task is difficult.

Accepting help or assistance

 Look at the person offering help.

 Sincerely thank him or her for helping.

 If help is not needed, politely decline the person's assistance.

 If help is needed, implement advice and again thank the person.

Accepting defeat or loss

 Look at the person or members of the team who won.

 Remain calm and positive.

 Say "Good game" or "Congratulations."

 Reward yourself for trying your hardest.

Accepting winning appropriately

 Look at the person or members of the team who lost.

 Remain pleasant but not overly happy or celebratory.

 Congratulate the other person or team for a good game and for trying.

 **Do not brag or boast about winning.**

Analyzing social situations

 **Look at the people you are getting ready to encounter.**

 Look at the situation that is occurring.

 Think about appropriate behaviors you have learned in the past.

 Choose the behaviors that seem the most appropriate for the situation and people you are dealing with.

Analyzing skills needed for different situations

 Look at the immediate situation facing you.

 Define the situation by what is occurring (i.e. people giving you criticism, instructions, introducing themselves, etc.).

 Match the curriculum skill to the situation (i.e. following instructions, accepting criticism, greeting skills, etc.).

 Perform the steps to the appropriate skill.

Analyzing tasks to be completed

 Clarify what task or assignment has been given to you.

 Begin listing every step that would need to be done in order for the task to be completed.

 Identify which step would need to occur first, second, third, etc.

 Begin completing the steps in order.

Appropriate clothing choice

 Think about what situations and activities you will engage in that day.

 Choose clothing that suits the season.

 Match colors and styles.

 Do not wear clothing that is too revealing or associated with gang activities.

 Care for your clothing throughout the day. Do not cut, tear, or write on clothing.

Being prepared for class

 Assemble all books, papers, homework, and writing implements.

 Be on time for class.

 Present homework and assignments when requested by the teacher.

 Write down assignments and homework to complete.

Borrowing from others

Make an appropriate request to borrow from another person.

Accept "No" if the person declines.

If the person agrees, find out when the possession being borrowed needs to be returned.

Promptly return others' property and care for belongings when you have them.

Care of others' property

 Use others' property only with their permission.

 Make an appropriate request.

 Use others' property only as it is intended to be used or according to instructions.

 Take care of others' property as if it was your own.

 If something gets broken, apologize and offer to replace it.

Care of own belongings

 Use your own property as it was intended to be used or according to instructions.

 Avoid needlessly tearing, writing on, or breaking your possessions.

 When you're done, return possessions to the appropriate place.

 If something gets broken, report it to an adult.

Choosing appropriate friends

 Think of the qualities and interests you would look for in a friend.

 Look at potential friends' strengths and weaknesses.

 **Match the characteristics of potential friends with activities and interests you would share.**

 Avoid peers who are involved with drugs, gangs, or breaking the law.

Complying with school dress code

 Know the clothing limits of your school.

 Choose clothing that matches those limits.

 Do not tear or write on your clothing at school.

 **Do not add or subtract clothing without telling the adults who are responsible for you.**

Compromising with others

 Identify disagreements before they get out of hand.

 **Suggest alternative activities that approximate both of what you and your peer desire.**

 Listen to what your peer suggests.

 **Remain calm and continue to compromise.**

Communicating honestly

 Look at the person.

 Use a clear voice. Avoid stammering or hesitating.

 Respond to questions factually and completely.

 Do not omit details or important facts.

 Truthfully admit to responsibility for any inappropriate behaviors you displayed.

Concentrating on a subject or task

 Promptly begin work on a task.

 Focus your attention directly on the subject.

 If your attention wanders, instruct yourself to concentrate on the task.

 Ignore distractions or interruptions by others.

 Remain on task until the work is completed.

Contributing to group activities

 Appropriately request to join in an activity.

 Ask what role you can play.

 Do your job thoroughly and completely.

 Cooperate with others by listening and accepting feedback.

 Praise others' performance and share credit for the outcome.

Controlling eating habits

 Eat mainly at mealtimes and limit between-meal snacks.

 Eat slowly, putting your knife and fork down between bites.

 Limit yourself to reasonable portions and few second helpings.

 Do not eat impulsively or when you are anxious or frustrated.

 Ask for help if eating habits get out of control.

Controlling emotions

Learn what situations cause you to lose control or make you angry.

Monitor the feelings you have in stressful situations.

Instruct yourself to breathe deeply and relax when stressful feelings begin to arise.

Reword angry feelings so that they can be expressed in a nonoffensive manner to others.

Praise yourself for controlling emotional outbursts.

Controlling sexually abusive impulses toward others

 Identify sexual feelings or fantasies about others as they occur.

 Instruct yourself to consider the consequences of acting on these impulses to you and the other person.

 Prompt yourself to not act on sexually abusive feelings. Remember what sexual abuse does to young children.

 Redirect your thoughts to other things or more appropriate behaviors.

 Ask for help with sexually abusive impulses.

Controlling the impulse to lie

 Identify untrue statements before you say them.

 Stop talking and pause.

 Answer all questions factually and make only truthful statements.

 Consider the long-term consequences of lying to others.

 Apologize for any untrue statements that were previously made.

Controlling the impulse to steal

 Identify and avoid situations in which you are likely to steal.

 Before you steal, stop your behaviors immediately.

 **Instruct yourself to leave the area without stealing.**

 **Consider the long-term consequences of stealing.**

 Self-report any previous stealing.

Cooperating with others

 Discuss mutual goals or tasks with others.

 Know what you must do to help accomplish those goals.

 Give and accept constructive criticism appropriately with peers.

 Follow rules if playing a game and share resources with others.

Praise peers' efforts and cooperation.

Coping with anger and aggression from others

 Look at the person.

 Remain calm and breathe deeply.

 Use a neutral voice and facial expression; no laughing or smirking.

 Avoid critical or sarcastic comments.

 Listen to and acknowledge what the other person is saying.

If the other person becomes aggressive or abusive, remove yourself from the situation.

 Report the incident to an adult.

Coping with change

 Identify exactly what is changing.

 Ask questions for clarification.

 Remain calm and relaxed.

Appropriately discuss feelings concerning the change with a caring adult.

 Avoid becoming unmotivated or depressed.

Coping with conflict

 Remain calm and relaxed.

 Listen to what the conflicting parties are saying.

 Think of helpful options.

 If appropriate, offer options to those people who are having a conflict.

If the situation becomes aggressive or dangerous, remove yourself.

Coping with sad feelings (or depression)

 Identify what situations tend to make you sad.

 Acknowledge sad feelings when they arise.

 Report your feelings to a caring adult or peer.

 Find alternative activities that you enjoy and engage in them. Get outside for fresh air and sunshine.

Avoid isolating yourself or withdrawing from friends and relatives.

 Discuss sad feelings openly and frankly.

Dealing with an accusation

 Look at the person with a neutral facial expression.

 Remain calm and monitor your feelings and behavior.

 Listen completely to what the other person is saying.

 Acknowledge what the person is saying or that a problem exists.

Ask if this is the appropriate time to respond. Say "May I respond to what you are saying?"

If the person says "Yes," then respond truthfully and factually by either self-reporting, peer reporting, or honestly denying the accusation.

If the person says "No," delay your appropriate disagreement to a later time and continue to listen and acknowledge.

Dealing with being left out

 Accurately identify that you have been left out or excluded.

 Remain calm and monitor your own feelings and behavior.

 Either find another positive activity to engage in or locate an adult to talk with.

Possibly discuss your feelings with those who initially left you out. Remember to give and accept criticism appropriately.

Dealing with boredom

 Identify the feeling of being bored.

 Look for alternative, appropriate activities.

 Request permission to engage in other activities.

 Avoid delinquent or gang-related behavior.

Dealing with contradictory messages

Identify which messages or people appear to contradict themselves.

Ask each person for clarification.

Specifically explain what messages appear contradictory.

Remember to continue following instructions and delay disagreements.

Dealing with embarrassing situations

 Think ahead to avoid as many embarrassments as possible.

 When embarrassed, remain calm and monitor your feelings and behavior.

 Continue to breathe deeply and relax.

 If possible, laugh at yourself and forget about the embarrassing situation.

 Otherwise, remove yourself from the situation in order to collect your thoughts and to relax.

Dealing with failure

Accurately identify that you did not succeed in a particular activity.

Remain calm and relaxed.

Instruct yourself to control emotional behavior.

Find a caring adult and discuss any negative feelings or your disappointment.

Be willing to try again to be successful.

Dealing with fear

 Identify what is making you afraid.

 Decide whether you are in danger or just feeling afraid or intimidated.

 Remain calm and relaxed. Continue to breathe deeply.

 Discuss with a caring adult what is causing your fear.

Instruct yourself to eventually conquer your fears.

Dealing with frustration

 Identify frustrated feelings as they arise.

 Learn the source of frustrated feelings.

 Breathe deeply and relax when frustrations arise.

 Discuss frustrations with a caring adult or peer.

Find alternative activities that promote feelings of success.

Dealing with group pressure

 Look at the group.

 Remain calm, but serious.

 Assertively say "No" to inappropriate group activities.

 Perhaps suggest an alternative activity.

 Remove yourself if pressure continues.

Dealing with rejection

 Examine behaviors that may have led to being rejected.

 Remain calm and relaxed.

 Use a neutral tone of voice with the other person.

 Possibly disagree appropriately or give appropriate criticism.

 If rejection continues, remove yourself and engage in alternative activities.

Decision-making

 Accurately identify what decision you must make.

 Examine what your choices currently appear to be.

 **Generate other choices, if possible.**

 **Look at the potential consequences (positive and negative) of each choice.**

 Pick the first- and second- best choices based on the potential outcomes.

Delaying gratification

 **Identify what you want or desire to do.**

 Instruct yourself to stop behaviors that are inappropriate to the situation.

 Remain calm and relaxed.

 Find alternative activities to substitute.

Displaying effort

 Remain on task and work diligently.

 Do your best to accomplish tasks to criteria.

Inform others of your efforts, if appropriate.

Expressing appropriate affection

 Identify the other person.

 **Decide on the appropriate boundary or level of closeness between you and the other person.**

 **Choose the appropriate behaviors to match that level of closeness and the situation.**

 Assess the other person's comfort with the situation and your affectionate behaviors.

 Refrain from overly physical displays of affection in public or with people you have only recently met.

Expressing feelings appropriately

 Remain calm and relaxed.

 **Look at the person you are talking to.**

 Describe the feelings you are currently having.

 Avoid statements of blame and profanity.

 Take responsibility for feelings you are having.

 Thank the person for listening.

Expressing optimism

 Look at the person.

 Use an enthusiastic voice tone.

 Describe potential positive outcomes.

 Express hope and desire for positive outcomes.

 Thank the person for listening.

Expressing pride in accomplishments

 Look at whom you are talking to.

 Use an enthusiastic voice tone.

 **Describe accomplishments and pride in them.**

 **Be careful not to brag, boast, or put down others.**

Following safety rules

 Learn the rules that apply to different situations.

 Adjust behaviors according to directives in rules.

 Do not "bend" or test safety rules.

 Report others who break safety rules, for their own good.

Following through on agreements and contracts

 Avoid making commitments you cannot keep.

 Know exactly what is involved in any agreements you make.

 Do exactly what you committed to do promptly and completely.

 If you cannot follow through, apologize and offer to compensate.

Giving instructions

 Look at the person you are instructing.

 Begin with "Please...."

 State specifically what you would like him or her to do.

 Offer rationales, if needed.

Thank the person for listening and for following your instructions.

Giving rationales

Look at the person.

Explain your point of view with rationales that the other person can understand.

Make your rationales point out the potential benefit to the other person.

Ask if the person understands your reasoning.

Interacting appropriately with members of the opposite sex

Decide what is the appropriate level or boundary that fits the relationship observing proper moral standards.

A boundary is an imaginary line that determines the amount of openness and sharing in a relationship.

In general, boundaries are intellectual, emotional, physical, and spiritual.

Avoid overly physical displays of affection.

Avoid jokes or language that is sexually oriented and may make the other person uncomfortable.

 Do not engage in inappropriate sexual behavior, which includes sexual intercourse, homosexual activity, incest, sexual activity with someone much older or younger, rape, violent intimidating boy-girl relationships, sexually taking advantage of another person, and overt public displays of affection, such as fondling and petting.

Keeping property in its place

 Know where property is usually kept or belongs.

 Ask the appropriate person for permission to remove property.

 Take care of property you are responsible for.

Return the property to its place in its original condition.

Lending to others

 If possible, respond to requests of others by saying "Yes."

 Only lend your property or those things for which you are responsible.

 Specify when you would like your property returned.

 Thank the other person for returning your property.

Making new friends

 Look at the potential new friend.

 Use a pleasant voice and introduce yourself.

 Share some of your interests and hobbies.

 Listen to the other person's name and areas of interest.

 Plan appropriate activities with permission.

Making restitution (Compensating)

 Begin by making an appropriate apology.

 Offer to compensate for any offenses you may have committed.

 Follow through on restitution promises.

 Thank the person for allowing you to make compensation.

Negotiating with others

1. Calmly explain your viewpoint to the other person.

2. Listen to the other person's ideas.

3. Offer an alternative or compromise that is mutually beneficial.

4. Give rationales for opinions.

5. Together choose the best alternative.

6. Thank the person for listening.

Meal-planning

 Know what food is available or make a grocery list.

 Plan meals based on the four food groups.

 Solicit opinions or feedback from roommates.

 Monitor contents of foods you buy. Avoid foods that are high in fats and carbohydrates.

Organizing tasks and activities

 List all tasks you are required to do.

 Prioritize tasks based on importance and your abilities and time.

Complete tasks in the order that they have been prioritized.

 Manage your time well and avoid putting off tasks until the last minute.

Persevering on tasks and projects

Know exactly what must be done in order to complete a task or project.

Get started promptly without procrastinating.

Remain on task until finished.

Deal appropriately with frustrations or disappointments.

Preparing for a stressful conversation

 Remember and practice relaxation strategies.

 **Instruct yourself to continue breathing deeply.**

 Remember to keep looking at the person and express your feelings appropriately.

Review skills such as accepting criticism, appropriate disagreement, and problem-solving.

Preventing trouble with others

 Identify situations that commonly result in conflicts.

 Review the skills necessary to handle those specific situations.

 Approach situations with a positive voice, smiles, and a willingness to compromise.

 Ask for advice from a caring adult.

Problem-solving a disagreement

 Look at the person.

 Remain calm. Use a pleasant voice.

 Identify options for solving the disagreement.

 Evaluate the potential consequences.

 Choose the best solution for the situation.

 Be open to views of the other person.

Relaxation strategies

 Breathe deeply and completely.

 Tighten and relax any tense body areas.

 Instruct yourself to remain calm.

 Visualize a relaxing scene (i.e. mountains, walking along a beach, etc.).

 At the first sign of increasing stress, say to yourself "3, 2, 1, relax" and continue breathing deeply.

Responding to complaints

Look at the person.

Remain calm.

Listen closely to the person's complaint.

Express empathy and acknowledge the problem.

If appropriate, apologize and attempt to correct the problem.

Delay disagreements until later.

Responding to others' feelings

 Listen closely to the other person.

 Acknowledge what he or she is saying and feeling.

 Express concern and empathy.

 Offer to help or provide advice, if wanted.

 Encourage the person to seek more help, if necessary.

Responding to others' humor

If the humor is appropriate, laugh accordingly.

If the humor is inappropriate, ignore it or prompt the person not to make such jokes.

If inappropriate humor continues, report the other person's behavior to an adult.

Responding to teasing

 Remain calm, but serious.

 Assertively ask the person to stop teasing.

 If the teasing doesn't stop, ignore the other person or remove yourself.

If the teasing stops, thank the other person for stopping and explain how teasing makes you feel.

 Report continued teasing or hazing to an adult.

Responding to written requests

 Read the request completely.

 Ask for clarification, if needed.

 Perform the requests promptly and thoroughly.

 Check back when the task is completed.

Self-advocacy

Identify a situation in which you should advocate for yourself.

Remember to remain calm and use a pleasant or neutral voice tone.

Describe your point of view or the outcome you desire.

Give rationales for advocating for yourself.

Thank the person for listening.

Self-correcting own behaviors

 Monitor your behaviors during difficult or stressful circumstances.

 Notice the effects your behaviors have on other people. Notice their response to what you say.

 Instruct yourself to correct behaviors that appear to make others uncomfortable.

 Use new behaviors and note their effects.

Continue to make adjustments, as necessary.

 **Reward yourself for correcting your own behaviors.**

Self-reporting own behaviors

 Find the appropriate person to report to.

 Look at the person.

 Remain calm and use a neutral voice tone.

Truthfully and completely describe your behaviors you are reporting.

 Honestly answer questions that you are asked.

Peer report, if necessary.

Avoid making excuses or rationalizing behaviors.

Self-talk or instruction

 Stop ongoing behaviors that are causing problems.

 Look at what is happening around you.

 Think of the best alternative behavior to engage in.

 Instruct yourself to engage in the appropriate alternative behavior.

 Reward yourself for self-talk.

Setting appropriate boundaries

 Imagine a series of circles radiating out from you. Each represents a boundary.

 People you encounter should be pictured in one of the circles, depending on the level of closeness with which you and the other person are comfortable.

 Disclose personal information only to those in the closest boundaries.

 Touch others only in ways that are appropriate to your boundaries. Also, respect the boundaries of others.

Sharing personal experiences

Decide if you should share personal experiences with the other person.

Notice if that person appears comfortable with what you are telling him or her.

Share experiences that are appropriate for another person to know.

Prompt the other person if what you told him or her is confidential.

Sharing attention with others

 Sit or stand quietly while sharing attention.

 Avoid distracting behaviors such as whining, laughing loudly, or complaining.

 Wait until the others pause.

 Contribute to the discussion or activity appropriately.

Spontaneous problem-solving

 Stop ongoing problem behaviors and relax.

 Define the immediate problem situation facing you.

 Think of alternative actions and strategies.

 Think of the possible consequences for each option.

 Choose the best strategy for avoiding trouble and helping the situation.

Use the best strategy and examine the outcome.

 Reward yourself for problem-solving.

Sportsmanship

 Play fair and according to the rules.

 Avoid fighting or criticizing others.

 Remember to accept winning appropriately without bragging.

 Remember to accept losing appropriately without pouting or complaining.

 Thank the other players for participating.

Study skills

Assemble necessary books and materials.

Focus your attention on the required academic work.

Make notes of important facts.

Repeat important points to yourself several times.

Remain on task, free from distractions (no radio or TV going).

Suggesting an activity

 Get the other person's attention.

 Suggest a specific activity or project to engage in.

 Give rationales for your ideas.

 Listen to the other person's opinions.

Time management

 List all tasks for a particular day or week.

 Estimate the time needed to complete each task.

 Plan for delays, setbacks, and problems.

 Implement a daily schedule that includes planned tasks.

 Evaluate your time management plan for effectiveness.

Use of appropriate humor

 **Use humor only under appropriate circumstances.**

 Avoid humor that makes fun of groups in society, handicapped people, or individuals in your peer group.

 Avoid sexually oriented jokes and profanity.

 If humor offends others, promptly and sincerely apologize.

Use of appropriate language

 Choose words that accurately reflect your thoughts and feelings.

 Avoid making blaming statements.

 Know the meaning of words and phrases you choose.

 Avoid profanity, slang, or terms that others may find offensive.

 Frequently ask if you are being clear and understood.

Working independently

 Start on tasks promptly without procrastinating.

 Remain on task without being reminded.

 Continue working unprompted until the task is completed.

 Check back with the person who assigned the task.

Accepting self

 Accurately identify your own strengths and weaknesses.

 Express appropriate pride in your accomplishments.

  Compensate for weaknesses by accentuating your strengths.

Use self-accepting phrases when talking about your tastes, style, etc.

Altering one's environment

 Identify situations in which you encounter difficulty.

 Look for pieces of those situations that could be changed (decorations, colors, clothing, etc.).

 Make changes to improve self-esteem, behavior, and performance.

Appropriate risk-taking

 Identify new activities that represent reasonable risks.

 Evaluate whether these risks could be dangerous or have negative consequences.

 If appropriate, try the new activity and do your best.

 Ask an adult's advice if you are unsure.

Asking for advice

 Locate a person who is qualified to give you advice.

 Ask if the person has time to talk.

 **Specifically describe the situation in which you need help.**

 Listen closely to the advice.

Thank the person for his or her time.

 If the advice appears useful, implement the suggestions.

Assertiveness

 Look at the person.

 Use a neutral, calm voice.

 Remain relaxed and breathe deeply.

 **Clearly state your opinion or disagreement. Avoid emotional terms.**

 Listen to the other person.

Acknowledge other viewpoints and opinions.

 Thank the person for listening.

Assessing own abilities

 Make a list of your strengths and weaknesses.

 List situations in which you have been successful or have had problems.

 Plan future activities in consideration of your abilities.

Being an appropriate role model

 Identify the situation as requiring appropriate modeling for younger peers or siblings.

 Engage in positive interactions with adults or peers. Only initiate appropriate conversation topics.

 Refrain from inappropriate language, sexual behavior, delinquency, bullying, etc.

 Correct peer behavior in a positive, constructive manner.

 Remember that inappropriate role-modeling is unfair to younger children.

Budgeting and money management

Assess your consistent weekly or monthly income.

List all of the bills or expenditures you have to make during the same time period.

Estimate the costs of appropriate leisure time activities and entertainment.

Set aside 10% of your income to be saved for unexpected needs or put into the bank.

Stay within the budget planning you have done.

 Refrain from impulsively spending money or writing checks.

Clarifying values and beliefs

 Decide what behaviors you consider appropriate and inappropriate.

 Learn how your behavior affects other people.

 Decide what characteristics about yourself you value and don't want to change.

 Decide if you have characteristics that you do not value and would like to change.

 Picture the type of person you want to be and how this would affect others.

Conflict resolution

 Approach the situation calmly and rationally.

 Listen to the other people involved.

Express your feelings appropriately and assertively.

 Acknowledge other points of view.

 Express a willingness to negotiate and compromise.

Help arrive at a mutually beneficial resolution.

 Thank the other person for cooperating.

Consumerism

 Know the contents of food and beverages you buy.

 Look for ways to save money with sales, store brands, etc.

 If a store sells you a defective product, return it and appropriately request a refund.

 Keep track of receipts, warranties, etc.

 Learn what rights consumers have.

Differentiating friends from acquaintances

 With each person you know, think about how long you have known him or her.

 Identify the activities you may engage in with either friends or acquaintances.

 Share personal information only with people you know as friends.

 Avoid compromising situations (i.e. accepting rides, dating, drinking) with people you have only known a short time.

Displaying appropriate control

 Monitor your feelings, and your verbal and non-verbal behavior.

 Use relaxation strategies to manage stress.

 Speak calmly, clearly, and specifically.

 Accurately represent your feelings with well-chosen words.

 Use language that will not be offensive to others.

Expressing empathy and understanding for others

 Listen closely to the other person's feelings.

 Express empathy by saying, "I understand...."

 Demonstrate concern through words and actions.

 Reflect back the other person's words by saying, "It seems like you're saying...."

 Offer any help or assistance you can.

Expressing grief

 Find an appropriate person to talk to.

 Discuss your feelings of grief.

 Feel free to cry or release hurt feelings as needed.

Ask for advice, if needed.

 Possibly seek professional assistance.

Formulating strategies

 Decide on the goal or product.

 Analyze the critical steps in accomplishing the goal.

 List any alternative strategies.

 Implement the best plan and follow through to completion.

Gathering information

 Know your topic or what you need information about.

 Go to the school or local library.

 Ask for help from reference staff.

 Assemble materials.

 Extract the information critical to the topic.

Goal-setting

Decide on overall values and lifestyle desires.

List the resources needed to fulfill these lifestyle options.

Examine the intermediate steps in accomplishing your overall outcome.

Establish short- and long-term goals that will accomplish all steps toward the desired outcome.

Identifying own feelings

 Examine how you are currently feeling.

 List how your feelings change with different situations and experiences.

 Monitor your body's feelings when you actually encounter these situations.

 Correctly identify and label various feelings as they arise.

 Communicate your feelings so they can be understood by others.

Interviewing for a job

 Dress neatly and appropriately for the job.

Introduce yourself enthusiastically to the interviewer.

 **Answer all questions honestly and calmly.**

Emphasize your strengths, as well as what you would still need to learn.

 **Ask any questions you have about the job at the conclusion of the interview.**

 Thank the person for his or her time.

Job-finding strategies

 Decide on the types of jobs you are qualified for.

 Look in the newspaper for current employment ads.

 Check the phone book for businesses where you can apply for a job. Start at their personnel offices.

 Check with adults you know about businesses they may be familiar with.

 Examine ads posted at local employment offices.

Laughing at oneself

Identify a situation that previously may have caused you embarrassment or discomfort.

Look for the humor in these situations.

Be willing to laugh at mistakes or imperfections.

Maintaining relationships

 Frequently ask for feedback and be willing to accept it.

 Express concern and appropriate affection.

 Negotiate and compromise on activities.

 Share attention with others and avoid possessive or exclusionary behaviors.

Making an appropriate complaint

 Look at the person.

 Phrase your complaint as an objective problem, not a personal attack.

 Remain calm and pleasant.

 Be assertive, but avoid repeating your complaint over and over.

 Thank the person for his or her cooperation.

Moral and spiritual decision-making

 Decide on values regarding life, sexuality, and intimacy.

 Remember that your values should be expressed in your behavior.

 Do not use people for your own personal or sexual gratification.

 Behave in ways that demonstrate your respect for fellow human beings and concern for their needs.

Patience

Sit or stand quietly.

Wait until your turn or you are called on.

Avoid making loud complaints or becoming angry.

Disagree appropriately later on.

Planning ahead

Know your eventual goal or outcome.

Identify in what sequence tasks or objectives need to occur.

Make plans for task completion that account for demands on your time.

Keep future plans flexible and able to be adapted to changing circumstances.

Recognizing moods of others

 Notice the situation that is occurring.

 Note the other person's facial expression, voice tone, and gestures.

 Think about what feelings you are experiencing when you demonstrate similar behaviors.

 Assess the other person's current mood or feelings.

 If possible, check out your assessment with him or her.

Resigning from a job or project

 Find out the required amount of notice to be given.

 Inform your supervisor calmly and pleasantly of your intention to resign.

 Give a positive reason.

 Always give at least the minimum amount of notice required.

 Avoid walking off of a job or leaving under negative circumstances.

Rewarding yourself

 Decide if what you have just done is praiseworthy.

 **If so, tell yourself you have done a good job and feel good about it.**

 Possibly give yourself an extra privilege or treat for a particular success.

Prompt yourself about your increasing competency and ability.

Seeking professional assistance

Decide if you are having a serious problem or crisis.

Identify the type of health care professional that can help you.

Locate one through referral by a professional you currently know or the phone book.

Specifically describe your problem to the person you go to for help.

Self-monitoring and reflection

 Think about behaviors you are engaging in and the feelings you are having.

 **Correctly identify and label your behavior and feelings.**

 Think about whether these are appropriate to the current situation.

 Identify alternative behaviors or skills that would be more productive.

Stress management

 Identify stress-producing circumstances.

 Learn your body's responses to stressful situations.

Use relaxation cues to overcome stress responses.

 **Generalize these relaxation cues to the situations that tend to cause stress.**

 Reward yourself for utilizing stress-management techniques.

Thought-stopping

 Identify negative or repetitive thoughts you wish to avoid.

 When these occur, consistently say to yourself, "Stop!"

 Immediately visualize a more positive scene or relaxing thought.

 Reward yourself for utilizing thought-stopping strategies.

Tolerating differences

 Examine the similarities between you and the other person.

 Take note of the differences.

 Emphasize the shared interests, tastes, and activities between you and the other person.

 Express appreciation and respect for the other person as an individual.

Use of leisure time

Engage in leisure time activities when tasks are completed and with permission.

Choose activities that are age-appropriate, healthy, and productive.

Develop new interests and hobbies whenever possible.

Avoid delinquent or gang-related activities.

Limit your TV consumption.

Look at resources in the community for entertainment and fun.

Utilizing community resources

 Establish exactly what your needs are.

 Use information numbers and directories to government agencies and services.

 Use directories for nonprofit agencies that may be able to assist you.

 Look in the newspaper listings under "community services" for additional resources.

 Utilize staff at public libraries.

Social skills grouped by behavior problems

▶ Depression and withdrawal problems

▶ Serious conflicts with authority figures

▶ Sexual behavior or identity problems

▶ Sexual perpetrator behavior

▶ Peer interaction problems

Skill No.   Skill Name, Location

2   Accepting "No" for an answer, page 61

3   Talking With Others, page 63

4   Introducing Yourself, page 65

5   Accepting Criticism or a Consequence, page 67

6   Disagreeing Appropriately, page 69

8   Showing Sensitivity to Others, page 77

9   Accepting Apologies from Others, page 79

10   Accepting Compliments, page 80

17   Appropriate Voice Tone, page 88

18   Appropriate Word Choice, page 89

27   Contributing to Discussions (Joining in a Conversation), page 98

31   Correcting Another Person (or Giving Criticism), page 102

34   Getting Another Person's Attention, page 105

36   Giving Compliments, page 107

38   Ignoring Distractions by Others, page 109

41   Listening to Others, page 112

42   Making an Apology, page 113

46   Participating in Activities, page 118

47   Personal Hygiene, page 119

50   Refraining from Possessing Contraband or Drugs, page 122

52   Reporting Other Youths' Behavior (or Peer Reporting), page 124

53   Resisting Peer Pressure, page 125

55   Saying "No" Assertively, page 127

63   Waiting Your Turn, page 136

66   Accepting Defeat or Loss, page 139

67   Accepting Winning Appropriately, page 140

69   Analyzing Skills Needed for Different Situations, page 142

73   Borrowing from Others, page 146

74   Care of Others' Property, page 147

76   Choosing Appropriate Friends, page 149

78   Compromising with Others, page 151

81   Contributing to Group Activities, page 154

88   Coping with Anger and Aggression from Others, page 161

93   Dealing with Being Left Out, page 169

96   Dealing with Embarrassing Situations, page 172

100   Dealing with Group Pressure, page 176

113   Interacting Appropriately with Members of the Opposite Sex, page 189

118   Negotiating with Others, page 195

124   Problem-Solving a Disagreement, page 201

127   Responding to Others' Feelings, page 204

129   Responding to Teasing, page 206

137   Sharing Attention with Others, page 216

139   Sportsmanship, page 219

150   Assertiveness, page 231

152   Being an Appropriate Role Model, page 234

167   Laughing at Oneself, page 250

168   Maintaining Relationships, page 251

180   Tolerating Differences, page 263

181   Use of Leisure Time, page 264

▶ School behavior and attendance problems

▶ **D**ishonesty or stealing behavior

▶ **I**mpulse control difficulty and attention deficits

▶ Chronic relocation and running away

▶ Low self-esteem

Skill No.   Skill Name, Location

▶ Drug and alcohol abuse

Social skills grouped by situations

▶ **Interactions with parents and family**

▶ Classroom behavior and academic performance

▶ Interpersonal conflict and disagreement

▶ Friendship and dating

▶ Transition to independent living

▶ ■ Interactions with supervisors and coworkers

Skill No.   Skill Name, Location

Social Skills Index

References

Adams, G.R., Openshaw, D.K., Bennion, L., Mills, T., & Noble, S. (1988). Loneliness in late adolescence: A social skills training study. **Journal of Adolescent Research, 3**, 81-96.

Cartledge, G., & Milburn, J.F. (Eds.) (1980). **Teaching social skills to children**. New York: Pergamon Press.

Combs, M.L. and Slaby, D.A. (1977). Social skills training with children. In B.B. Lahey and A.E. Kazdin (Eds.), **Advances in clinical child psychology** (pp. 161-201). New York: Plenum Press.

Cruickshank, W.M., Morse, W.C., & Johns, J.S. (1980). **Learning disabilities: The struggle from adolescence toward adulthood.** Syracuse, NY: Syracuse University Press.

Elder, J.P., Edelstein, B.A., & Narick, M.M. (1979). Adolescent psychiatric patients: Modifying aggressive behavior with social skills training. **Behavior Modification, 3**, 161-178.

Father Flanagan's Boys' Home (1991). **The Boys Town Family Home Program Training Manual.** Boys Town, Nebraska: Father Flanagan's Boys' Home.

Filipczak, J., Archer, M., & Friedman, R.M. (1980). In-school social skills training: Use with disruptive adolescents. **Behavior Modifica-tion**, 4, 243-263.

Friedman, R.M., Quick, J., Mayo, J., & Palmer, J. (1983). Social skills training within a day treatment program for emotionally disturbed adolescents. In C. LeCroy (Ed.), **Social skills training for children and youth** (pp. 139-151). New York: Haworth Press.

Goldstein, A.P., Sprafkin, R.P., Gershaw, N.J., & Klein, P. (1980). The adolescent: Social skills training through structured learning. In G. Cartledge and J.F. Milburn (Eds.), **Teaching social skills to children** (pp. 249-279). New York: Pergamon Press.

Gresham, F.M. (1981). Social skills training with handicapped children: A review.

Review of Educational Research, 51, 139-176.

Hains, A.A., & Hains, A.H. (1988). Cognitive-behavioral training of problem-solving and impulse-control with delinquent adolescents. **Journal of Offender Counseling, Services and Rehabilitation,** 12, 95-113.

Hansen, D.J., St. Lawrence, J.S., & Christoff, K.A. (1988). Conversation skills of inpatient conduct-disordered youths: Social validation of component behaviors and implications for skills training. **Behavior Modification, 12,** 424-444.

Hansen, D.J., St. Lawrence, J.S., & Christoff, K.A. (1989). Group conversation-skills training with inpatient children and adolescents: Social validation, generalization, and maintenance. **Behavior Modification, 13,** 4-31.

Hazel, J.S., Schumaker, J.B., Sherman, J.A., & Sheldon-Wildgen, J.S. (1983). Social skills training with court-adjudicated youths. In C. LeCroy (Ed.), **Social skills training for children and youth** (pp. 117-137). New York: Haworth Press.

Hendrick, C. (1988). Social skills: A basic subject. **Academic Therapy,** 23, 367-373.

Howing, P.T., Wodarski, J.S., Kurtz, P.D., & Gaudin, J.M. (1990). The empirical base for the implementation of social skills training with maltreated children. **Social Work, 35,** 460-467.

Jones, M.B., & Offord, D.R. (1989). Reduction of antisocial behavior in poor children by nonschool skill development. **Journal of Child Psychology and Psychiatry, 30,** 737-750.

Kazdin, A.E. (1985). **Treatment of antisocial behavior in children and adolescents.** Homewood, IL: The Dorsey Press.

LeCroy, C.W. (1983). Social skills training with adolescents: A review. In C. LeCroy (Ed.), **Social skills training for children and youth** (pp. 117-137). New York: Haworth Press.

Long, S.J., & Sherer, M. (1984). Social skills training with juvenile offenders. **Child and Family Behavior Therapy, 6,** 1-11.

Moyer, J., & Dardig, J.C. (1978). Practical task analysis for special educators. **Teaching Exceptional Children, 3,** 16-18.

Oden, S. (1980). A child's social isolation: Origins, prevention, intervention. In G. Cartledge and J.F. Milburn (Eds.), **Teaching social skills to children** (pp. 179-202). New York: Pergamon Press.

Patterson, G.R. (1982). **Coercive family process.** Eugene, OR: Castalia.

Peter, V.J. (1986). **What makes Boys Town so special.** Boys Town, NE: Father Flanagan's Boys' Home.

Schinke, S.P., Gilchrist, L.D., & Small, R.W. (1979). Preventing unwanted adolescent pregnancy: A cognitive-behavioral approach. **American Journal of Orthopsychiatry, 49,** 81-88.

Shivrattan, J.L. (1988). Social interactional training and incarcerated juvenile delinquents. **Canadian Journal of Criminology, 4,** 145-163.

Sulzer-Azaroff, B., & Mayer, G.R. (1986). **Achieving educational excellence using behavioral strategies.** New York: Holt, Rine-hart and Winston.

Svec, H., & Bechard, J. (1988). An introduction to a metabehavioral model with implications for social skills training for aggressive adolescents. **Psychological Reports, 62,** 19-22.

Trower, P., Bryant, B., & Argyle, M. (1978). **Social skills and mental health.** Pittsburgh: University of Pittsburgh Press.

Veneziano, C., & Veneziano, L. (1988). Knowledge of social skills among institu-tionalized juvenile delinquents. **Criminal Justice and Behavior, 15,** 152-171.